Contents

	Page
List of figures, tables and maps	vi
List of contributors	xi
Acknowledgements	xii
Introduction	xiii

Chapter 1: Families

Introduction	**2**
Families in context	**2**
Households, families and children	**2**
Families with children	4
Stepfamilies	5
Dependent children	5
Age variations for families and children	**6**
Age distribution of family reference person	6
Family types	6
Ages of dependent children	8
Families in households	**8**
Multi-generational households	9
Ethnicity of multi-generational households	9
Other extended family households	10
Non-family households	**10**
Communal establishments	10
Children not in families	11
Family formation and change	**12**
Women under the age of 25	12
Men and women aged 35 to 39	12
Marriage	13
Divorce and separation	14
Cohabitation	14
Same-sex partnerships	16
Notes and references	**16**

Page

Chapter 2: Unpaid care and the family

Introduction   **20**
Numbers and characteristics of people providing unpaid care   **20**
    Numbers and types of unpaid carers   20
    Characteristics of unpaid carers   21
Marital and cohabitation status and provision of unpaid care   **22**
    Legal marital status and provision of unpaid care   22
    De facto marital status and provision of unpaid care   23
The family type of carers   **24**
    Married and cohabiting couple families   24
    Married couple families with and without children   25
    Older people and spouse care   26
    Lone parent families and co-resident care for parents   26
    Older people not in a family and intergenerational care   28
Minority ethnic groups and the provision of unpaid care   **30**
Issues in the provision of unpaid care and the family   **32**
    The health of unpaid carers   32
    Provision of unpaid care and economic activity   32
    Changing family forms and the future of unpaid care   33
Notes and references   **34**

Chapter 3: Family structure and family formation – education as outcome and explanation

Introduction   **36**
PART ONE: Family type and educational outcomes   **36**
    Couples, parents and qualifications   36
    Educational outcomes among 17-year-olds   37
    Children in education   37
    Qualifications   38
    Findings from previous studies   40
Stepfamilies   **40**
    Children in education   40
    Qualifications   41
    Gender differences in education   42
Socio-economic differences   **43**
    Children in education   43
    Gender differences in education   44
    Gender differences in qualifications   46
**Overall differences between the proportions with qualifications
and in full-time education**   **46**
PART TWO: Education and marital formation   **47**
    Highest level of qualifications and marriage or cohabitation by given ages   47
    Ever married   49
    Single (never married) and cohabiting   50
    Single (never married) and not cohabiting   51
Conclusions   **52**
    Educational outcomes and family type   52
    Education and marital formation   52
Notes and references   **53**

FOCUS ON Families

2007 edition

Editors: Steve Smallwood
Ben Wilson

First published 2007 by
PALGRAVE MACMILLAN
Houndmills, Basingstoke, Hampshire RG21 6XS and 175 Fifth Avenue, New York, NY 10010, USA
Companies and representatives throughout the world.

PALGRAVE MACMILLAN is the global academic imprint of the Palgrave Macmillan division of St. Martin's Press, LLC and of Palgrave Macmillan Ltd. Macmillan® is a registered trademark in the United States, United Kingdom and other countries. Palgrave is a registered trademark in the European Union and other countries.

ISBN 978-1-4039-9323-6 ✓

This book is printed on paper suitable for recycling and made from fully managed and sustained forest sources. Logging, pulping and manufacturing processes are expected to conform to the environmental regulations of the country of origin.
A catalogue record for this book is available from the British Library.

10 9 8 7 6 5 4 3 2 1
16 15 14 13 12 11 10 09 08 07

Printed and bound in Great Britain by
Hobbs the Printers Ltd,
Totton, Hampshire.

A National Statistics publication

National Statistics are produced to high professional standards set out in the National Statistics Code of Practice. They are produced free from political influence.

About the Office for National Statistics

The Office for National Statistics (ONS) is the government agency responsible for compiling, analysing and disseminating economic, social and demographic statistics about the United Kingdom. It also administers the statutory registration of births, marriages and deaths in England and Wales.

The Director of ONS is also the National Statistician and the Registrar General for England and Wales.

Contact points

For enquiries about this publication, contact the editor, Steve Smallwood.

Tel: 01329 813539
Email: steve.smallwood@ons.gsi.gov.uk

For general enquiries, contact the National Statistics Customer Contact Centre.

Tel: 0845 601 3034 (minicom: 01633 812399)
E-mail: info@statistics.gsi.gov.uk
Fax: 01633 652747
Post: Room 1015, Government Buildings,
          Cardiff Road, Newport NP10 8XG

You can also find National Statistics on the Internet at:
www.statistics.gov.uk

Publication orders

To order a copy of *Focus on Families* or any other Palgrave Macmillan publication call 01256 302611 or order online at:
www.palgrave.com/ons

Page

Chapter 4: Family living arrangements and health

Introduction   **56**
Definitions   **56**
Health and family – previous findings   **56**
Sex differences in relationships between marital status and health   56
Age differences in relationships between marital status and health   57
Household size and structure and other types of living arrangements   57
Divorce and family health   57
Children and family health   57
Family and health in 2001   **59**
Data Sources   59
Health and living arrangements: measures available   59
Mortality by marital status   59
Self-reported morbidity by marital status   61
Alternative measures of health   62
Morbidity by family status   63
Morbidity of children by family status   65
**Explanations for the observed relationships: selection, protection
and stress effects**   **66**
Selection effects   66
Protective effects   66
Stress of bereavement or marital breakdown   67
Conclusion   **67**
Notes and references   **67**

Chapter 5: Family geography

Introduction   **72**
Maps   **72**
Families in the UK   **73**
Family type by country and GOR   73
Children in families   73
Dependent children by Local Authority District and Council Area   **76**
Married couples with dependent children   78
Cohabiting couples with dependent children   78
Families with out dependent children   **78**
Lone parent families with non-dependent children only   78
Cohabiting couples with non-dependent children only   80
Families with three or more dependent children   **80**
Stepfamilies   **80**
Stepfamilies with dependent children   82
Married stepfamilies with dependent children   82
Stepfamilies with some children of both partners   83
Multiple family households   **84**
Lone parent families in multiple family households   85
Notes and references   **86**

Appendix   87

Glossary   93

List of figures, tables and maps

Page

1. Families

Figure 1.1	Households and families, 1971 to 2006	3
Figure 1.2	All families: by family type, 1996 and 2006	3
Table 1.3	All families: by family type and presence of children, 2001	4
Figure 1.4	Number of cohabiting couples, 2001	5
Table 1.5	Dependent children: by family type, 2006	5
Table 1.6	All families: by age of family reference person, 2001	6
Figure 1.7	Family age distributions, 2001	7
Figure 1.8	Families with dependent children: by age of youngest child and family type, 2001	8
Table 1.9	Household composition, 1991 and 2001	9
Figure 1.10	Multi-generational households as a proportion of family households: by ethnic group of household reference person, 2001	9
Figure 1.11	Proportion of people not in a family but related to at least one other person in the household: by household type, 2001	10
Figure 1.12	Marital status of men and women (aged 16 or over): by residential status, 2001	11
Figure 1.13	Experience of family events by women before the age of 25: by age, 2001–2003	12
Figure 1.14	Marital and partnership status of men and women aged 35 to 39 by year of birth, 1931–1970	13
Figure 1.15	Percentage of individuals married at survey by age at survey and year of birth, 1946–1960	14
Figure 1.16	Percentage of individuals divorced or separated (and not cohabiting) at survey by age at survey and year of birth, 1946–1960	14
Figure 1.17	Percentage of individuals cohabiting at survey by age at survey and year of birth, 1946–1960	15
Figure 1.18	Percentage of individuals cohabiting at survey by age at survey and year of birth, 1966–1980	15

2. Unpaid care and the family

Table 2.1	Provision of unpaid care by adults: by relationship of care-recipient to carer and hours of care, 2000/01	21
Table 2.2	Provision of unpaid care by adults: by locus of care and hours of care, 2000/01	21
Figure 2.3	Percentage of adults who provide care for one or more hour(s) per week: by age, 2001	21

Page

Figure 2.4   Percentage of adults who provide care for twenty hour(s) per week or more: by age, 2001   21

Figure 2.5   Percentage of adults who provide care for one or more hour(s) per week: by gender and ten-year age bands, 2001   22

Table 2.6   Percentage of adults who provide care for one or more hour(s) per week: by legal marital status, gender and age, 2001   22

Table 2.7   Percentage of adults who provide care for twenty or more hour(s) per week: by legal marital status, gender and age, 2001   23

Figure 2.8   Percentage of adults who provide care for one or more hour(s) per week: by partnership status and 5-year age bands, 2001   23

Figure 2.9   Percentage of adults who provide care for twenty or more hour(s) per week: by partnership status and 5-year age bands, 2001   23

Figure 2.10   Percentage of adults who provide care for twenty or more hour(s) per week: by partnership status, legal marital status of those not in couples and age bands, 2001   24

Table 2.11   Percentage of adults who provide care for twenty or more hour(s) per week: by family type and age, 2001   24

Figure 2.12   Family type of adults providing care for one or more hour(s) a week: by age bands, 2001   25

Figure 2.13   Family type of adults providing care for twenty hours a week or more: by age band, 2001   25

Figure 2.14   Family type of adults providing care for one or more hour(s) a week: by presence of children in family and by age band, 2001   26

Figure 2.15   Family type of adults providing care for twenty or more hours a week: by presence of children in family and by age band, 2001   26

Figure 2.16   Provision of care for twenty hours a week or more by adults: by family type, relationship of care-recipient to and age band, 2000/01   27

Figure 2.17   Provision of care for twenty hours a week or more by people aged 65 and over in married couple families without children: by gender and age band, 2001   27

Figure 2.18   Percentage of adults who provide unpaid care for twenty hours a week or more in lone parent families: by gender and age band, 2001   28

Figure 2.19   Family type of people aged 65 and over: by age band, 2001   28

Figure 2.20   Family type of people aged 85 and over by provision of unpaid care and hours of care provided, 2001   28

Table 2.21   Reported source of help for people with a functional disability, aged 60 and over: age band, 2002/03   29

Figure 2.22   Provision of unpaid care by adults aged 16 and over: by relationship of care-recipient to carer, 5-year age bands, 2000/01   29

Figure 2.23   Provision of unpaid care for twenty hours a week or more by married adults: gender and 5-year age bands, 2001   29

Table 2.24   Provision of unpaid care by adults: by ethnic group, hours of unpaid care and gender, 2001   30

Page

Figure 2.25   Percentage of adults who provide unpaid care for one hour a
week or more: by ethnic group and age band, 2001   31

Figure 2.26   Percentage of adults who provide unpaid care for twenty hours
a week or more: by ethnic group and age band, 2001   31

Figure 2.27   Family type of adults providing unpaid care for twenty hours
a week or more: by ethnic group, 2001   31

Figure 2.28   Percentage of adults with a limiting long-term illness: by age
band and hours of caring, 2001   32

Figure 2.29   Provision of unpaid care for one hour a week or more by
adults below state retirement age: by gender and economic
activity, 2001   32

Figure 2.30   Provision of unpaid care for twenty hours a week or more by adults
below state retirement age: by gender and economic activity, 2001   33

Figure 2.31   Cohabiting population aged 16 and over by age, 2002–2031   33

3. Family structure and family formation – education as outcome and explanation

Table 3.1   Highest level of qualification of Family Reference Person and
partners according to family type and presence or absence of
dependent/non-dependent children, 2001   36

Figure 3.2   Total number and proportion of single individuals who are not
lone parents, are aged 17, and are living within families, by
family type, 2001   37

Figure 3.3a   Single individuals who are not lone parents, are aged 17, and
are living within families by family type and sex: percentages
in full-time education, 2001   38

Table 3.3b   Single individuals who are not lone parents, are aged 17, and
are living within families by family type and sex: percentages
in full-time education, 2001   38

Table 3.4   Family type by age for children living with a parent or parents,
2001   38

Table 3.5   Qualifications at Level 2 or higher for individuals aged 17:
by family type and sex, 2001   39

Table 3.6   Student status of 17-year-olds in stepfamilies according to family type,
stepchild status and sex, 2001   41

Table 3.7   Percentage of 17-year-olds in stepfamilies with qualifications at
Level 2 or higher according to family type, stepchild status and
sex, 2001   42

Figure 3.8   Difference between female and male children in percentage
points, 2001   42

Figures 3.9   Percentage of children (male and female) aged 17 in full-time
education according to family type and household NSSEC, 2001   43

Table 3.10   Differences between the percentages of female and male children
aged 17 in full-time education according to family type and
household NSSEC band, 2001   44

Page

Figures 3.11   Percentage of children (male and female) aged 17 with qualifications at Level 2 or higher according to family type and household NSSEC, 2001   45

Table 3.12   Differences between the percentages of female and male children aged 17 with qualifications at Level 2 or higher according to family type and household NSSEC band, 2001   45

Figures 3.13   A comparison for 17-year-olds (male and female) between the percentage in full-time education and the percentage with qualifications at Level 2 or higher, 2001   46

Table 3.14   Highest level of qualifications by sex for individuals aged 25, 35 and 45, 2001   48

Figures 3.15   Percentage of men and women ever married according to highest level of qualifications for three age cohorts, 2001

Figures 3.16   Percentage of men and women who are currently cohabiting but never married according to highest level of qualifications for three age cohorts, 2001   50

Figures 3.17   Percentage of men and women who are never married and are not currently cohabiting according to highest level of qualifications for three age cohorts, 2001   51

4. Family living arrangements and health

Table 4.1   Definition of alternative indicators of health   60

Table 4.2   Ratio of mortality rates by sex and age group of the single, widowed and divorced to that of married people, average over period 2002–2004   60

Figure 4.3   Proportion of males and females with long-term illness by marital status, 2001   61

Table 4.4   Proportion of people in communal establishments by age, sex and marital status, 2001   62

Figure 4.5   Proportion of males and females with long-term illness by marital status and type of residence, 2001   63

Table 4.6   Relative risk of health problem by marital status (married = 1), by age and sex, 2001   64

Figure 4.7   Proportion of males and females with long-term illness by family type, 2001   64

Table 4.8   Relative risk of health problem by family type (with partner and no child(ren) = 1), by age and sex, 2001   65

Table 4.9   Relative risk of limiting long-term illness among children 0–15 by family type (with both natural parents = 1), by age and sex, 2001   65

5. Family geography

Table 5.1   Proportion of families by type for each region (country or Government Office Region), 2001   72

Map 5.2   Proportions of families in each region: lone parent families, stepfamilies, married and cohabiting couple families, 2001   74

Page

Map 5.3   Proportions of families in each region: families with no children, with non-dependent children only, with one dependent child, and with three or more dependent children, 2001   75

Map 5.4   Lone parent families with dependent children as a proportion of all families with dependent children, 2001   76

Map 5.5   Married couple families with dependent children as a proportion of all families with dependent children, 2001   77

Map 5.6   Cohabiting couple families with dependent children as a proportion of all families with dependent children, 2001   77

Map 5.7   Lone parent families with non dependent children only as a proportion of all families with non dependent children only, 2001   79

Map 5.8   Cohabiting couple families with non dependent children only as a proportion of all families with non dependent children only, 2001   79

Map 5.9   Families with three or more dependent children as a proportion of all families with dependent children, 2001   81

Table 5.10   Proportion of stepfamilies according to stepchild status by Government Office Region and country, 2001   81

Map 5.11   Stepfamilies with dependent children as a proportion of all families with dependent children, 2001   82

Map 5.12   Married stepfamilies with dependent children as a proportion of all stepfamilies with dependent children, 2001   83

Map 5.13   Stepfamilies with some children of both partners together as a proportion of all stepfamilies, 2001   84

Map 5.14   Families in multiple family households as a proportion of all families, 2001   85

Map 5.15   Lone parent families in multiple family households as a proportion of all lone parent families, 2001   86

List of contributors

Authors:	Hannah McConnell	(ONS)
	Linda Pickard	(London School of Economics)
	Richard Lampard	(Warwick University)
	Mike Murphy	(London School of Economics)
	Ben Wilson	(ONS)
	Steve Smallwood	(ONS)
Editorial team:	Steve Smallwood	
	Ben Wilson	
	Diana Shaw	
Typesetting:	ONS Design	

Acknowledgements

The editors wish to thank the authors who have all contributed so much time and energy to *Focus on Families*. Special thanks also go to our colleagues in the Office for National Statistics (ONS) for their invaluable support in the preparation of this report. In particular, we would like to thank John Haskey and Hannah McConnell, who did a large amount of work to plan, organise and prepare for *Focus on Families*.

We are grateful to our colleagues at the General Register Office for Scotland and Northern Ireland Statistics and Research Agency. Finally, we are also grateful to the time given by authors from whom chapters had been planned but whose work we were unable to publish in this volume.

Introduction

Focus on Families provides an up-to-date and comprehensive description of families at the start of the 21st century. It presents a wealth of information on families, how they have changed over time and the demographic forces driving these trends.

One of the central questions at global, national and sub-national levels is how life varies according to the family type in which you live. For example, do different family types vary according to health, education or care provision for their members?

An understanding of families is crucial for those involved in planning and decision making at the national and local level. Moreover, at one time or another, every member of society is part of, or affected by, his or her family situation.

The following chapters bring together data from a variety of sources to describe the characteristics of UK families. Where possible, the report covers the population of the UK as a whole, and includes geographical variations in family characteristics.

The report is aimed at people who want to deepen their understanding of the UK's families, be they students, teachers, researchers, policy makers or members of the general public. It is designed to be accessible to a general audience, with text, charts, maps and tables that are easy to understand, and an appendix for those who want more information on data and methods.

The structure of *Focus on Families* is as follows:

Chapter 1, Families, gives an overview of the UK's families and how they have changed over time. It describes the main family types and explores the presence of children in UK families. Less common family types are also explained, including stepfamilies and extended families. The chapter also explores multi-generational and non-family households and then concludes by examining variations in family formation and change for different generations.

Chapter 2, Unpaid care and the family, examines family variations in the provision of unpaid care. The 2001 Census was the first to collect information on the provision of unpaid care in the population. As such, this chapter takes advantage of census coverage to explore the marital status and family type of those who care. Additional dimensions are explored, including age and ethnicity, before the author concludes with a discussion of key issues relating to unpaid care and families in the UK today.

The middle chapter is **Chapter 3, Family structure and family formation – education as outcome and explanation**, and is split into two parts. The first part looks at the relationship between family type and educational outcomes. It considers the specific case of 17-year-olds in 2001, whether they are in full-time education and the highest level of qualifications that they obtain. Education and marital formation is the focus of the second part of the chapter, which explores how marital status varies according to highest level of qualifications. The chapter concludes by evaluating the results and comparing with the latest academic research.

Chapter 4, Family living arrangements and health, considers the relationship between family living arrangements and health, including a review of the relationship between marital status, family living arrangements and health. Analyses are presented on mortality by marital status, on variations in self-reported long-term illness from the 2001 Census, and across a number of different indicators of health status – self-reported and independently-measured – from the 2001 Health Survey for England.

Finally, **Chapter 5, Family geography**, provides an overview of geographical variations in family types across the UK. This chapter uses census data, which provides a rare opportunity to accurately examine family geography. The first half of the chapter shows geographical variations for the main family types, lone parent, cohabiting and married couple families. Geographical variations for stepfamilies and multiple-family households are explored in the second half.

More information on the data and classifications used in this report can be found in the **Appendix** and **Glossary**.

Focus on Families is part of the 'Focus on' series of publications from the Office for National Statistics (ONS). The series combines data from the 2001 Census and other sources to illustrate various topics, and provides links to further information. Other reports in the series cover the digital age, environmental accounts, ethnicity and identity, gender, health, London, older people, religion, social inequalities, Wales and people and migration. Each report consists of a short overview of the topic, followed by a full report containing more comprehensive analysis. The overviews and full reports can be viewed or downloaded from the National Statistics website:

www.statistics.gov.uk/focuson

Families

Hannah McConnell and Ben Wilson

Chapter 1

Introduction

This chapter provides a brief overview of one of the most intricate and extensive topics in demography, the family. Providing a framework for the other analyses in this volume, the first section concentrates on the demographic characteristics of contemporary families. The chapter then looks at family trends, including marriage, divorce and cohabitation, and considers how household and family formation have changed over time.

Most of us live in families and most of us live in households containing one family. Many of these are 'traditional' families of a married couple with children, but increasingly people are experiencing family life within a cohabiting couple or a lone parent family. The recent patterns of family dynamics – the decline and delay of marriage and childbearing, and the increase in divorce, cohabitation and births outside marriage – also mean that individuals are more likely to experience a greater variety of family structures throughout their lifetimes. Consequently there is an increasing minority who live in 'reconstituted' families as family units break up and reform.

Families in context

It is important to distinguish between a 'family' and a 'household'. In general standard definitions are used throughout this report (Box 2), although definitions may vary slightly between sources (Box 1). A household may contain one family or more. In addition, it may contain household members other than those in the family (such as other relatives or friends). In many cases, a household may not contain any families, with the most common type of non-family household being a one-person household.

Where no family data are available, household data can provide a valuable insight into families, but it is important to be aware of the differences in definitions between the two. Communities and Local Government (CLG) is responsible for producing household estimates and projections and information focused on households is available from CLG (**www.communities.gov.uk**). Of particular interest are the Housing and Households[6] report based on 2001 Census data and the Household and population estimates and projections.[7]

Households, families and children

In 2006 there were 17.1 million families in the UK, over 2 million more families in the UK than in 1971 (Figure 1.1). Over the same period the number of households increased by 6 million to 24.9 million. The growing trend in people living alone accounted for much of the increase in the number of households and, as a result, the average household size has declined.

Box 1

Data sources

Reporting of family statistics is mainly carried out on an ad hoc[1,2] or survey specific[3,4] basis. Some publications, such as *Social Trends*[5], do include regular items related to household composition.

The census and most government surveys – notably the General Household Survey (GHS) and the Labour Force Survey (LFS) – collect statistical data on households and their members. As a result, in reporting families there are a number of different sources available, each with their own purpose and advantages.

Data from the LFS provides a large sample of all people in households. It therefore enables UK-wide coverage of all major family types. The LFS has provided full and comprehensive family data since 1996 when the relationship matrix was introduced.

Conducted since 1971, the GHS is a survey of Great Britain. It provides a longer time series of households and families data than the LFS, albeit for a smaller sample of the population of Great Britain. The family information section of the GHS, which is currently asked of all sampled 16 to 59-year-olds, allows more detailed analysis to be carried out, such as analysis of stepfamilies or relationship histories.

The census can be used for more detailed analysis, such as analysis by lower level geography (below Government Office Region, for example at county, borough or ward level), age and ethnic group. More detailed breakdowns of family types (such as the age and number of children) are also possible and it provides UK coverage for most variables. In Great Britain the 1961 Census was the first to satisfactorily distinguish families from households and in Northern Ireland the first report on household composition was published for the 1971 Census.

In addition to the above data sources, 'best estimates' have periodically been made of key statistics such as the number of lone parent families, children in lone parent families and the population cohabiting. At the time of producing this volume, work is underway to update these estimates. Where appropriate, other data sources, such as registration data, have been used to illustrate the trends and patterns influencing family and household formation.

Box 2

Definitions and Explanations

Family: a married or cohabiting couple with or without child(ren) or a lone parent with child(ren). Child(ren) may be dependent or non-dependent.

Dependent children: children living with their parent(s) aged under 16, or aged 16 to 18 in full-time education, excluding all children who have a spouse, partner or child living in the household.

Non-dependent children: children aged 16 and over living with their parent(s) who have no spouse, partner or child living in the household (excludes those aged 16 to 18 in full-time education).

Household: a person living alone, or a group of people living at the same address who either share one main meal a day or share the living accommodation (or both).

These definitions are based on 2001 Census classifications. Definitions between sources are broadly similar. See the Glossary for notes on any variation between data sources.

When other related people live together: Members of some households may be related to each other as siblings, cousins, aunts, uncles, nieces, nephews or in other ways. To be considered a family within the census definition, however, they would need to fit into one of the categories above – for example, a married or cohabiting couple or parent(s) and child(ren) living together.

In 2006 more than two thirds of households in the UK contained one or more families, with the largest proportion consisting of just one family. In 2006, just 1 per cent of households in the UK (0.2 million) were multiple-family households while in 1971, the equivalent figure was 2 per cent. This decline can be partly attributed to an increase in the provision of first public, and then private, housing in the 1970s and 1980s.[8]

Figure 1.2 shows the composition of the UK's families by family type for 1996 and 2006. Between these years, the number of families has increased by 4 per cent, but the rise in the number of families has not been uniform across all types.

Approximately 7 in 10 families were headed by a married couple in 2006. However, the proportion of married couple families has declined, with a corresponding rise in cohabitation and lone motherhood. Between 1996 and 2006 the number of married couple families fell by over 4 per cent (0.5 million). The number of cohabiting couple families increased by over 60 per cent to 2.3 million, while the number of lone mother families increased by over 11 per cent, also to 2.3 million (lone mothers with dependent and non-dependent children). Children in lone parent families continue to be more likely to live with their mother than with their father. In 2006 nearly nine out of ten lone parents were lone mothers. Nevertheless, the prevalence of lone fatherhood as a proportion of all families has remained fairly constant since 1996 at almost 2 per cent. These trends are a continuation of those recorded for Great Britain in the late 1980s and early 1990s.[2]

Figure **1.1**

Households and families, 1971 to 2006

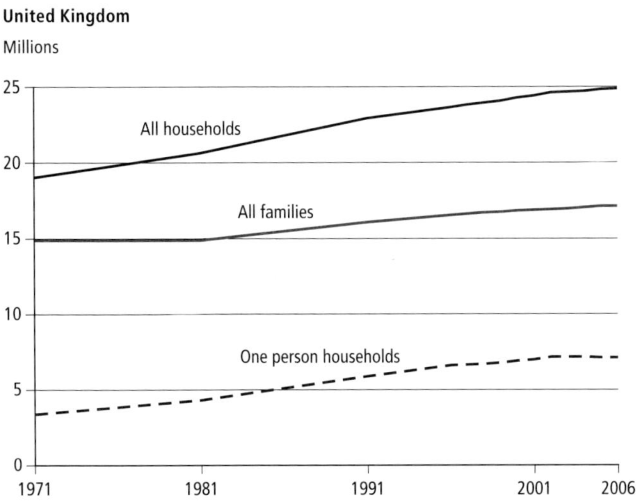

United Kingdom

Millions

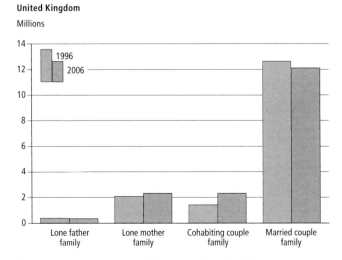

Source: Censuses, Office for National Statistics; Censuses, General Register Office for Scotland; Censuses, Northern Ireland Statistics and Research Agency; Household estimates, Communities and Local Government; Household estimates, Scottish Executive; Labour Force Survey, Office for National Statistics

Figure **1.2**

All families: by family type, 1996 and 2006

United Kingdom

Millions

Source: Labour Force Survey, Office for National Statistics

Families with children

Using data from the 2001 Census, Table 1.3 shows the number of families according to family type and the presence of children. In 2006, 43 per cent of UK families had no children and 14 per cent had only non-dependent children. Cohabiting couples were more likely to have no children than married couples, 57 per cent compared with 50 per cent. However, the proportion of families with dependent children was almost the same for cohabiting and married couples, 39 per cent and 38 per cent respectively. By definition, there were no lone parents without children. Nevertheless, there was a marked difference between lone mothers and lone fathers. For the UK, 73 per cent of lone mothers had dependent children, whereas the same figure for lone fathers was 50 per cent. Lone fathers were more likely to have non-dependent children only.

The proportions by family type are very similar for England, Scotland and Wales. Within cohabiting families, Scotland and Wales have smaller proportions of families with no children, 53 per cent (for both) compared with 57 per cent for the UK overall. Otherwise, only Northern Ireland is considerably different from the other constituent countries, with 49 per cent of families having dependent children, compared with 43 per cent for the UK. Correspondingly, only 33 per cent of families in Northern Ireland had no children in the household compared

Table **1.3**

All families: by family type and presence of children, 2001

United Kingdom   Numbers

	England	Wales	Scotland	Northern Ireland	United Kingdom
Total Families	13,845,301	835,680	1,422,212	442,584	16,545,777
with no children	5,768,679	337,616	562,900	126,862	6,796,057
with dependent children	6,010,686	364,584	616,391	228,933	7,220,594
with non-dependent children only	2,065,936	133,480	242,921	86,789	2,529,126
Married couple family	9,727,670	589,984	998,743	324,610	11,641,007
with no children	4,638,981	284,534	469,010	111,807	5,504,332
with dependent children	3,797,233	221,463	381,123	159,241	4,559,060
with non-dependent children only	1,291,456	83,987	148,610	53,562	1,577,615
Married couple stepfamily	*431,846*	*26,894*	*33,927*	*9,483*	*502,150*
with no children	*-*	*-*	*-*	*-*	*-*
with dependent children	*325,237*	*20,583*	*24,305*	*7,208*	*377,333*
with non-dependent children only	*106,609*	*6,311*	*9,622*	*2,275*	*124,817*
Cohabiting couple family	1,901,138	99,753	163,432	26,842	2,191,165
with no children	1,129,698	53,082	93,890	15,055	1,291,725
with dependent children	699,154	42,720	62,441	10,624	814,939
with non-dependent children only	72,286	3,951	7,101	1,163	84,501
Cohabiting couple stepfamily	*321,268*	*18,573*	*29,403*	*4,658*	*373,902*
with no children	*-*	*-*	*-*	*-*	*-*
with dependent children	*269,262*	*15,922*	*24,249*	*3,895*	*313,328*
with non-dependent children only	*52,006*	*2,651*	*5,154*	*763*	*60,574*
Lone mother family	1,910,554	126,275	226,526	79,611	2,342,966
with no children	-	-	-	-	-
with dependent children	1,361,279	90,746	157,615	54,441	1,664,081
with non-dependent children only	549,275	35,529	68,911	25,170	678,885
Lone father family	305,939	19,668	33,511	11,521	370,639
with no children	-	-	-	-	-
with dependent children	153,020	9,655	15,212	4,627	182,514
with non-dependent children only	152,919	10,013	18,299	6,894	188,125

Note: The numbers presented here may vary from other census outputs because of changes relating to disclosure and confidentiality.

Source: 2001 Census, Office for National Statistics; General Register Office for Scotland; Northern Ireland Statistics and Research Agency

with 43 per cent for the UK. Additionally, the proportion of families headed by a cohabiting couple in Northern Ireland (7 per cent) was half that of the UK (14 per cent).

Stepfamilies

Recent demographic changes and research[1, 9] suggest that the proportion of stepfamilies has increased. With the increase in divorce and lone parenthood since the 1960s, relatively more children are living in an increasing number of family types during their childhood[10] and this includes stepfamilies. However, reliable data on the prevalence of stepfamilies over time is sparse, particularly because of the small sample sizes involved. Prior to the 2001 Census, the GHS was the only source that routinely reported on stepfamilies, with information on stepmothers and stepfathers being collected since 1991.

The 2001 Census was the first census to allow the identification of stepfamilies. The census identified that there were 0.7 million stepfamilies with dependent children living in households in the UK – 0.4 million were married couple stepfamilies and 0.3 million were cohabiting couple stepfamilies. Additionally, there were 0.2 million stepfamilies with non-dependent children only (Table 1.3).

In 2001, there were 2.2 million cohabiting couples, of which 0.4 million were stepfamilies. Figure 1.4 shows the number of cohabiting couples according to their stepfamily status and the presence of dependent or non-dependent children. It confirms that cohabiting stepfamilies are more likely to include non-dependent children only. Note that, by definition, stepfamilies must include children.

Figure **1.4**

Number of cohabiting couples, 2001

United Kingdom

Numbers

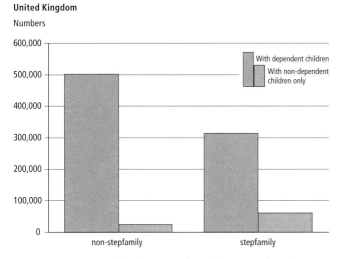

Source: 2001 Census, Office for National Statistics; General Register Office for Scotland; Northern Ireland Statistics and Research Agency

Dependent children

In 2006, there were 7.4 million families with dependent children in the UK. The total number of dependent children living in these families was 13.0 million, resulting in an average of 1.8 dependent children per family (this covers families with dependent children only; it is not an average of children among all families). Table 1.5 presents the number of dependent children by family type and shows that the majority, 65 per cent, of children lived in a married couple family. However, nearly 1 in 4 dependent children lived in lone parent families in 2006. This is substantially different from 1972, when the equivalent proportion was 1 in 14.[11]

In 1971, the average number of dependent children in a family was 2.0[10], noticeably different from the 1.8 mentioned above for 2006. It is interesting to note that these numbers are similar to the total fertility rates for the same periods.[12] Since fertility rates are a measure of births in a particular year, it is reasonable to assume that the main reason for the decrease in children per family is a decrease in UK fertility rates. To accurately explore the connection between fertility and family size, however, would require further analysis.

In recent years, despite the slight increase in the number of families with dependent children, the number of dependent children living in such families has fallen (from 13.3 million in 1996). This drop is largely because of the decline in the number of married couple families with dependent children. Married couple families were generally larger than other family types, with an average 1.8 dependent children in 2006, compared with 1.6 in cohabiting couple families, 1.7 in lone mother families and 1.4 in lone father families.

Comparing the four constituent countries of the UK, families in Northern Ireland were larger than elsewhere in the UK, and were more likely to contain dependent children. In 2006, 21 per cent of families with dependent children in Northern Ireland had three or more dependent children compared with 16 per cent for the UK as a whole.

Table **1.5**

Dependent children: by family type, 2006

United Kingdom

	Thousands	Percentages
Married couple family	8,420	65
Cohabiting couple family	1,492	12
Lone mother family	2,812	22
Lone father family	238	2
All dependent children in families	12,963	100

Note: Numbers may not add up because of rounding

Source: Labour Force Survey, Office for National Statistics

Age variations for families and children

Age distribution of family reference person

In order to analyse families by age, the age of the family reference person has been used as a proxy for the age of the family (Box 3). Therefore, in this section, when discussing young or old families, it is appropriate to remember that it is only the age of the family reference person that is being considered.

The proportions of each type of family vary with age according to trends that are discussed elsewhere in this chapter. It is particularly important to consider the variations illustrated here alongside those presented in the section titled 'Family Formation and Change' (later in this chapter).

One substantial variation that may not be obvious from the analysis elsewhere is the change in the total number of families by age. Clearly, this has an effect on the calculated proportions. Table 1.6 shows the total number of families by age of family reference person. As well as highlighting the variation in the numbers of families at younger ages, it shows the large difference between families aged 70 to 74 years old, and those aged 75 to 79 years old.

Table **1.6**

All families: by age of family reference person, 2001

United Kingdom

	Total Families	Percentage
16–19	62,147	0.4
20–24	417,677	2.5
25–29	1,063,415	6.4
30–34	1,757,612	10.6
35–39	2,057,330	12.4
40–44	1,925,013	11.6
45–49	1,734,484	10.5
50–54	1,852,993	11.2
55–59	1,509,410	9.1
60–64	1,179,033	7.1
65–69	1,030,135	6.2
70–74	1,107,343	6.7
75–79	333,897	2.0
80+	515,268	3.1
All families	16,545,757	100.0

Note: Families headed by people aged 16 and over in Great Britain and all families in Northern Ireland.

Source: 2001 Census, Office for National Statistics; General Register Office for Scotland; Northern Ireland Statistics and Research Agency

Box 3

Reference person

The UK Census 2001 used a family or household reference person to identify families and households and their characteristics. They are defined as follows:

Family Reference Person (FRP): In a lone parent family the FRP is taken to be the lone parent. The FRP in a couple is based on economic activity, then age (oldest), then the first member of the couple on the census form. In 2001 most FRPs were men – of FRPs aged 16 and over, 80 per cent of FRPs in married couple families and 73 per cent of FRPs in cohabiting couple families were men. Of lone parents, 14 per cent were lone fathers.

Household Reference Person (HRP): A person living alone is the HRP. If the household contains only one family (with or without ungrouped individuals) the HRP is the same as the FRP. If there is more than one family in the household or if there is no family in the household, the HRP is chosen from among the FRPs or individuals using the same criteria as for choosing the FRP.

Family types

Figure 1.7a shows the distribution of families across age groups for each family type. Generally, cohabiting couple families are much younger than married couple families. In 2001, half of cohabiting couple families in the UK were headed by a person aged under 35, compared with just over a tenth of married couples. The distributions of lone parent families are similar in shape, but lone mother families tend to be younger than lone father families by approximately ten years. 1 in 3 lone mothers in the UK was aged under 35, whereas fewer than 1 in 10 lone fathers were under 35.

Figure 1.7b shows the age distribution for families with and without children. Families with dependent children were more likely to be headed by a younger person than families with non-dependent children or no children living with them. Over 60 per cent of families with dependent children were headed by a person in their 30s or early 40s, whereas 55 per cent of families with non-dependent children (only) were headed by an adult in their late 40s or 50s.

Among families with no children living with them, cohabiting couples tended to be younger than married couples (Figure 1.7c). The fact that cohabitation is more prevalent at younger ages reflects both the fact that cohabitation is often a precursor to marriage and a greater acceptance of cohabitation among younger generations. Marriage being more prevalent at older ages is partly caused by the same factors, and partly a result of

Figure **1.7a**

All families: age distribution by family type, 2001

United Kingdom
Percentages

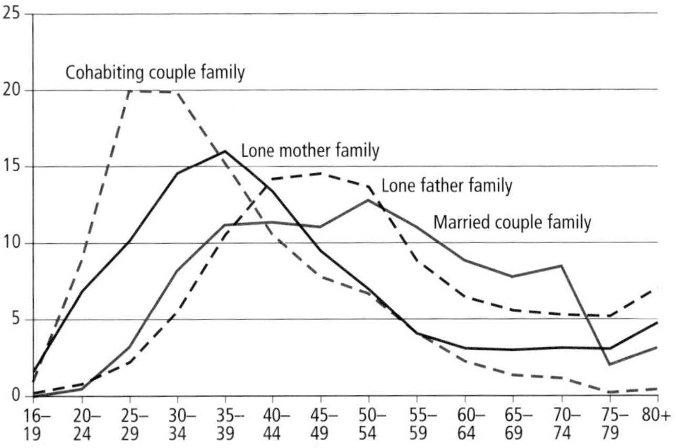

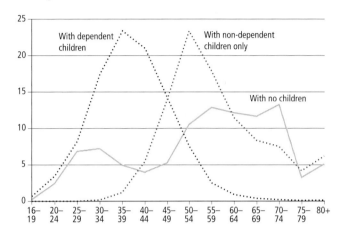

Figure **1.7b**

All families: age distribution by presence of children, 2001

United Kingdom
Percentages

Figure **1.7c**

Couple families with no children: age distribution, 2001

United Kingdom
Percentages

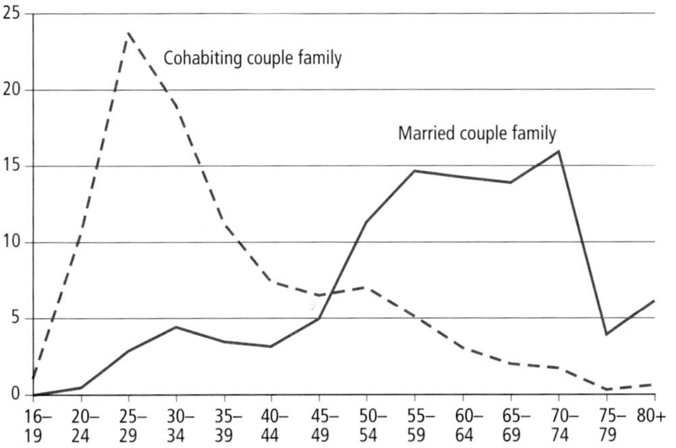

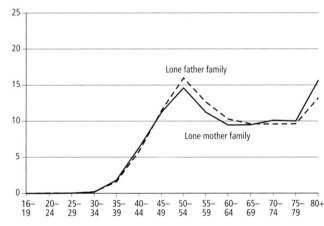

Figure **1.7d**

Lone parent families with non-dependent children: age distribution, 2001

United Kingdom
Percentages

Note: Families headed by people aged 16 and over in Great Britain and all families in Northern Ireland.

Source: 2001 Census, Office for National Statistics; General Register Office for Scotland; Northern Ireland Statistics and Research Agency

the higher marriage rates for older generations.[13,14] Overall, half of couple families with no children were aged 55 to 74 and nearly all of these were married couple families.

The age distribution of all stepfamilies followed the general trend for 2001. In other words, cohabiting couple stepfamilies had a younger age distribution than married couple stepfamilies. For married couple families with dependent children, the age distribution was very similar for both step and non-stepfamilies, whereas stepfamilies were slightly older than non-stepfamilies for cohabiting couple families with dependent children.

Figure 1.7d shows the age distribution for lone parent families with non-dependent children. Given that non-dependent children are older than dependent children, it is unsurprising that the age distribution is concentrated around older ages. Particularly noticeable is the larger proportion of lone parents over 80 years old. This is mainly a result of the age group over 80 containing a greater age range than the five-year categories. Overall, there are a larger number of families in this category (approximately 515,270) compared with those in the 75 to 79-year-old category (333,900).

A number of parents may become lone parents at older ages because of the death of their partner or their partner moving into communal care establishments. However, in order to be a lone parent family, the remaining partner must live with their child(ren). These are likely to be adult children who remain or return to live with their parent for care reasons (parent caring for child or child caring for parent). Care and the family are discussed in Chapter Two of this *Focus on Families* volume. Only 8.3 per cent of families aged 70 to 74 years old are lone parent families, while the equivalent figure for 75 to 79-year-olds is 27.1 per cent (for those over 80 years old the figure is 26.7 per cent). This difference reflects a reduction in the proportion of married couple families and the reduction in the overall number of families as mentioned above and shown in Table 1.6.

Ages of dependent children

Figure 1.8 shows the proportion of families for each family type according to the age of the youngest child in the family. This illustrates that children in families headed by lone fathers tend to be older than children in other types of families. In 2001, 60 per cent of (youngest) children in lone father families were over 10 years old. The equivalent figure for married couple and lone mother families was less than 40 per cent.

Cohabiting couples had the largest proportion of young children. Only 20 per cent of (youngest) children were over 10 years old. This pattern reflects the younger age structure of cohabiting couple families and the tendency for marriage to follow a period of cohabitation and family formation. Over 50 per cent of (youngest) children are 0 to 4 years old in cohabiting families. There is a considerable difference, not shown in Figure 1.8, between cohabiting stepfamilies and cohabiting non-stepfamilies. For the former, 36 per cent of (youngest) children are aged 0–4, whereas in cohabiting non-stepfamilies 69 per cent of (youngest) children are aged 0–4. A similar difference exists for married couple families, but it is only 14 percentage points.

Families in households

Several non-family categories can be used to classify households by the number and types of families present. Since households contain combinations of families and non-families, the variety of household types is much more numerous (Box 4).

Table 1.9 provides a summary of household types for 1991 and 2001 taken from census data for both years. The 2001 Census allowed new categories to be created for multiple families and the presence of others in the household (ungrouped individuals who are classified as 'not in a family'). However, less than 1 per cent of households in England and Wales comprised two or more families in both 1991 and 2001.

Overall, the proportion of family households decreased between 1991 and 2001, from 70.6 per cent to 67.0 per cent, a drop of 3.6 percentage points. This decrease was offset by a 3.9 percentage point increase in the proportion of one-person households over the same period. The greatest percentage change for family households was for those with one family with no others, which decreased by 2.9 percentage points.

Figure 1.8

Families with dependent children: by age of youngest child and family type, 2001

United Kingdom

Percentages

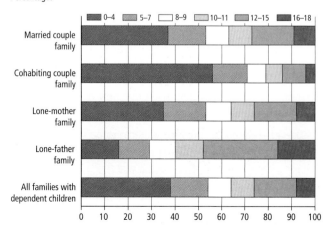

Source: 2001 Census, Office for National Statistics; General Register Office for Scotland; Northern Ireland Statistics and Research Agency

Box 4

Household types

Households with more than one person can include:

- one family

- and/or ungrouped individuals who may or may not be related to each other

- and any additional families in the household

An extended family household is defined as one containing two or more people who are related, but not categorised as living in the same family.

A multi-generational household is an extended family household that contains:

- three or more generations if it includes a lone parent family or a couple with children

- two generations including a couple with no children

Table **1.9**

Household Composition, 1991 and 2001

England and Wales

Percentages

	1991	2001
One-person household	26.1	30.0
Pensioner[1]	14.9	14.4
Other	11.2	15.6
Family households	70.6	67.0
One family and no others	66.2	63.3
One family with others	3.4	2.9
Two or more families and no others		0.7
Two or more families with others	0.9	0.1
Multi-person household	3.3	3.0
All student[1]	0.3	0.4
Other[1]	3.0	2.6
All Households	100	100

1 Figures for 1991 are estimates based on the 1991 Census

Source: 1991 and 2001 Census, Office for National Statistics

Households consisting of one family living with others accounted for 2.9 per cent of households in 2001, a slight decline from 3.4 per cent in 1991. These 'others' may be related to the family in some way and form an extended family household. There may also be relationships between household members in multi-person households, for example siblings or cousins living together without their parents.

Multi-generational households

The census relationship question improved with the introduction of the relationship matrix in 2001 (see Glossary). Outside of the family, however, it is still difficult to identify precise relationships between all members of a household (particularly large households). It is possible, though, to look at some extended family household types through identification of the number of generations of direct descent in a household. This enables advancement in identifying one type of extended family – a multi-generational household.

In 2001, 2.3 per cent of all households (family and non-family) in England and Wales were multi-generational households. As might be expected, households with a larger number of families are more likely to be multi-generational households. Over 70 per cent of households containing two or more families were multi-generational.

Family households headed by a married couple stepfamily or by a lone parent were the most likely to be a multi-generational

household, 7.1 and 5.0 per cent respectively. It might be expected that lone parents would live with other generations. For example, large proportions of young lone parents (aged 19 or under) live in a multi-generational household. These are likely to be lone parents living with their own parent(s). In the case of married couple stepfamilies living with other generations, it is families headed by an older person (aged 60 and over) that are more likely to live in multi-generational households.

Ethnicity of multi-generational households

It is known that Asian households are generally larger than households headed by someone of any other ethnic group.[15] Furthermore, households with an HRP (Box 3) of Asian origin are the most likely to be multi-generational households. Figure 1.10 shows the percentage of family households that are multi-generational households by ethnic group. Multi-generational households accounted for 14 per cent of households headed by someone of Pakistani, Bangladeshi or Indian ethnic background. In contrast, of all White households only 3 per cent were multi-generational.

These findings reflect differing demographic structures and family cultures of ethnic groups. Among all families, those headed by a person of non-White ethnic background were more likely than White families to have children living in them. Also, older people from non-White ethnic groups tend to live in larger households than those from the White population. In particular, Asian households are less likely to be one person

Figure **1.10**

Multi-generational households as a proportion of family households: by ethnic group of household reference person, 2001

England and Wales

Percentages

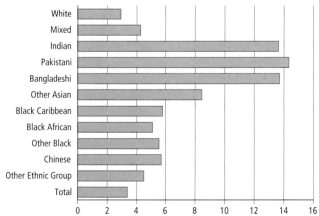

Note: Figures include grandparent families who are categorised as three generations.

Source: 2001 Census, Office for National Statistics

households when compared with White households and are the most likely to contain two or more families.[16] Older Asian people are the least likely to live alone or in communal establishments.[17,18] More information on ethnicity is available in *Focus on Ethnicity and Religion.*[16]

Other extended family households

Beyond multi-generational households, extended family households can consist of other relatives living together in non-family households or with a family unit. For example, a lone mother living with a sibling, or the families of two cousins living together. It is not possible to identify all specific relationships through the data available from the census, but some relationships between people can be recognised.

In 2001 most people not living alone in households lived with a least one person they were related to. Approximately 94 per cent of the population in households of two or more people lived with at least one relative, and the great majority of these were living in a family. However, some were classified as 'not in a family', and were living as an ungrouped individual in a family or multi-person household. One third of all people 'not in a family' live with at least one person they are related to. Figure 1.11 shows the proportions by household type.

An extended family household is defined as one containing two or more people who are related, but not categorised as living in the same family. Unsurprisingly, households already containing a family are more likely to be extended family households. Over half of people (54 per cent) who were living in one family households, but not in a family, were related to at least one other person in the household. Relatively few households are three or more family households, but in these households 70 per cent of non-family members were related to other household members.

In multi-person households, individuals were less likely to live with other relatives. Only 22.6 per cent of multi-person households contained a family relationship. In particular, multi-person student households were the least likely to contain extended families.

Those not in a family but living with other relatives are more likely to be older people. Over two-thirds of pensioners who are not in a family lived with other relatives compared with a quarter of non-pensioners. Those households containing pensioners not in a family may also be multi-generational family households as older people are more likely to be the parent and/or grandparent of someone in the household.

Figure **1.11**

Proportion of people not in a family but related to at least one other person in the household: by household type, 2001

England and Wales
Percentages

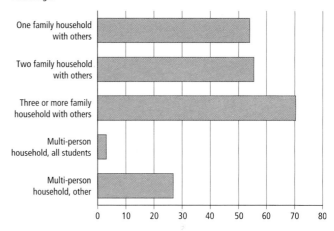

Source: 2001 Census, Office for National Statistics

Non-family households

As shown previously (Table 1.9), 30 per cent of households were one-person households in 2001 and by definition these are not families. In 2005 there were an estimated 7.1 million people living alone in the UK, twice as many as in 1971. The rise in the proportion of one-person households has slowed in recent years, but continues nonetheless. In 1971 in Great Britain, the proportion was 17 per cent, and by 1991 it reached 26 per cent. By 2005, the proportion of households that were one-person households was 31 per cent.[3]

The rise in one-person households has been driven by the number of working-age adults living alone. The change for people aged 60 or over has been less marked. In 1971, 12 per cent of all households contained only one adult aged 60 or over. By 2005 the equivalent figure was 15 per cent. Conversely, in 1971 5 per cent of households contained only one adult aged 16 to 59. In 2005 the proportion had increased to 16 per cent.

A small proportion of households consisted of two or more people who were either unrelated or were related but did not form a family. These multi-person households accounted for 3 per cent of households in the UK in 2005 compared with 4 per cent in 1971 (see Table 1.9 for 1991 and 2001 figures).

Communal establishments

In addition to the non-families above, a small proportion of the UK population are resident in communal establishments. In 2001, 1.0 million people (or 1.8 per cent of the population) in the UK were living in communal establishments. These include people living in residential care homes, students living in halls of residence, hotel staff living at the hotel, and those in prison or people staying in hostels (including people sleeping rough). Of the total, less than 50,000 were under 16 years old.

In the 2001 Census, family and relationship information for people living in communal establishments was not collected. However, the marital status of staff and residents was recorded. Figure 1.12 shows the marital status of men and women (16 or over) living in communal establishments, compared with those living in households.

Men and women living in communal establishments are more likely to be single or widowed than the general household population, who are more likely to be married. Over 70 per cent of men in communal establishments were single and men in communal establishments were twice as likely to be single and three times more likely to be widowed as compared with men in households. For women in communal establishments, around 90 per cent were either single or widowed (almost 45 per cent for each group). Nearly twice as many women in communal establishments were single and four times as many were widows as compared with women in households.

The marital status of individuals is influenced by the age and sex structure of the communal establishment population in which they reside. For example, students living in educational establishments are predominantly young and are therefore more likely to be single. Men considerably outnumber women in both defence and prison service establishments and, in general, these communal populations are also young.

On the other hand, those in medical and care establishments are more likely to be older, accounting for the larger proportions of widowed people in communal establishments than in households. In addition, the widowed population is much larger for women, partly reflecting the higher life expectancy of women than men in the UK. More detail on communal establishments and the people living in them can be found in *Focus on People and Migration*.[19]

Children not in families

Like adults, some children do not live in families at all. In 2001, 139,000 children were living in non-family households in the UK, this includes living with adults or other relatives who are not their parents (although grandparent families are included as families in certain circumstances – see Glossary). An additional 52,000 children under 16 lived in communal establishments such as children's homes.

Children waiting for adoption living in communal establishments are not included in the family statistics. However, once they have been adopted they will be recorded as a child in their new family. Over 6,000 children under 18 were adopted in the UK in 2005,[20] compared with 6,700 in 1996. The majority of these adoptions were in England and Wales (5,582 in 2005), where the proportion of children aged 1 to 4 when adopted increased from just over a quarter in 1996 to a half in 2005. Over the same period there were steady decreases in the proportions of children who were adopted when they were aged 5 to 9 and 10 to 14, while the proportion of adopted children under 1 was almost constant.

Figure **1.12**

Marital status of men and women (aged 16 or over): by residential status, 2001

United Kingdom

Percentages

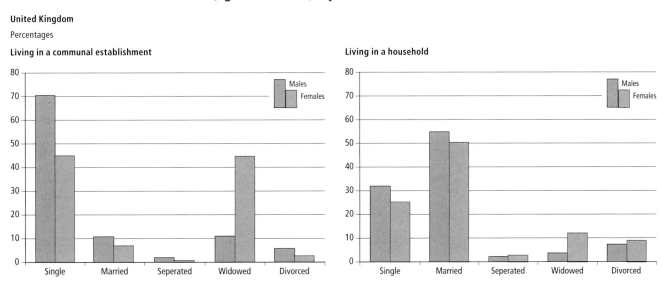

People living in communal establishments include all residents, staff and their families.

Source: 2001 Census, Office for National Statistics; General Register Office for Scotland; Northern Ireland Statistics and Research Agency

Family formation and change[21]

The current distribution of family types in the UK is the result of major changes in the nature and rate of change in family formation and dissolution, particularly since the beginning of the 1970s. Generally, lone parent and cohabiting couple families have increased, while married couple families have declined. A number of demographic trends have influenced families and households in recent times, most notably: the decline and delay of marriage and childbearing; the rise in divorce; the increase in cohabitation and the rise in births outside marriage.[12]

Women under the age of 25

Figure 1.13 looks at some of these family events for Great Britain by charting the proportion of women who had experienced different family events before the age of 25. For example, the results for 50-year-old women relate to events that occurred over 25 years ago. It is important to note that the more recent experiences are shown on the left-hand side. For example, marriage is lower in recent times. This is in contrast to most charts, where time increases on the right-hand side of the chart. The results are for all women, except for the results for marital breakdown, which are calculated as a proportion of those women who were married before the age of 25.

For women aged 25 to 29 at the time of interview, around a quarter were married before the age of 25. This compared with nearly three quarters of women aged 55 to 59. Similarly, less

than a third of women aged 25 to 29 had given birth before the age of 25 compared with over half of women aged 55 to 59.

The proportion of women aged 25 to 29 who had cohabited before the age of 25 was 21 per cent. For their counterparts who were aged 25 thirty years earlier (50–59 in Figure 1.13), the proportion was just 1 per cent. Increasing cohabitation does not fully account for the decline in marriage as a smaller proportion of women aged 25 to 29 had formed any union, either married or cohabiting, before the age of 25. This suggests a delay in partnership formation for younger generations of women.

For those women who did marry, the trend in women's experience of marital breakdown (either separation or divorce) has increased. More than double the proportion of women aged 25 to 29 had experienced marital breakdown before the age of 25 compared with women aged 55 to 59. Despite this, there is little difference in experience of marital breakdown for women aged 25 to 44. This suggests that the proportions of people who are divorced and separated have become more stable (allowing for annual fluctuations).

Men and women aged 35 to 39

The experiences of women in Great Britain before the age of 25 give a strong indication of a number of trends. However, the median ages of first marriage have increased in England and Wales from 24.0 (males) and 21.6 (females) in 1961 to 30.4 (males) and 28.3 (females) in 2004.[22] As such, younger generations are less likely to be exposed to marriage and other significant life events until they are in their thirties. Figure 1.14 shows the marital status of men and women aged 35 to 39 for different years of birth.

Before interpreting the analysis presented in Figure 1.14, some explanation is needed of how the information was constructed from the GHS survey data for Great Britain. The results are for individuals who were aged 35 to 39 **when they were surveyed**, meaning that the information is collected over a long time period. For example, the information for the 1946–50 generation comes from the 1981 to 1989 surveys. The generations shown at the beginning and end of the table only contain partial information. Those born 1931–35 would theoretically have been surveyed between 1966 (1931+35) and 1974 (1935+39). In fact, the GHS started in 1971 so only information from 1971–74 is used, thus weighting the results for these generations towards the earlier born in the generation. Conversely, the results for the latest generations (1966–1970) are weighted towards the later born.

Figure 1.14 confirms that the proportion of 35 to 39-year-olds who are married has declined in recent years. The difference between individuals born 1946–50 and 1961–65 is 20.3

Figure **1.13**

Experience of family events by women before the age of 25: by age[1], 2001–2003[2]

Great Britain

Percentages

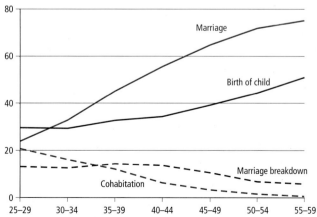

1 Age at time of interview.
2 Combined years: 2001, 2002 and 2003.

Source: General Household Survey, Office for National Statistics

Figure **1.14**

Marital and partnership status of men and women aged 35 to 39 by year of birth, 1931–1970

England and Wales

Percentages

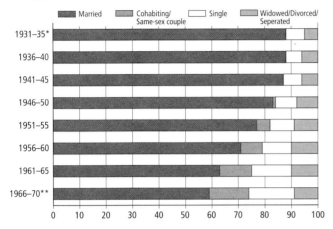

Note: Cohabitation and same-sex questions were not established for men and women born before 1946.

* For year of birth 1931–35 the sample does not have complete coverage for all age and year combinations, because the GHS survey did not begin until 1972.
** For year of birth 1966–70 the sample does not have complete coverage for all age and year combinations, because this would require GHS results up to and including 2009.

Source: GHS Time Series Dataset (1972–2004)

percentage points. Looking at the rest of the figure, this difference appears to be made up by individuals either cohabiting or remaining single. Comparing the same groups – those born 1946–50 with 1961–65 – there was a 10.8 percentage point rise in the proportion cohabiting and a 7.0 percentage point rise in the proportion remaining single. The remaining change over the same period was in the proportion separated, increasing by 1.6 percentage points. It is still not possible to tell whether these changes can be accounted for by delays in marriage and partnership formation in general or a decision not to partner at all.

Looking at the categories not shown separately, there was a 4.2 percentage point increase in the proportion of divorced individuals (aged 35–39), comparing those born in 1931–1935 with 1951–55. While many individuals will divorce after they are 39 years old, these results reflect the general increase in divorce that occurred from 1961 to 1981.[22] The Divorce Reform Act 1969 came into affect in 1971 which may partly explain the increase in divorce between those born in 1931–35 and those born in later years. In 1984 the Matrimonial and Family proceedings act was passed allowing couples to divorce after only 12 months of marriage. This may partly explain the increase between those born in 1941–45 and those born in later years. For those born most recently, after 1951, the proportion divorced has stabilised at around 6 per cent.

Comparing those born in 1931–35 and those born in 1966–70, the proportion separated increased by 1.4 percentage points and the proportion widowed decreased by 0.9 percentage points. Changes in the proportion separated are likely to be related to changes in the proportion divorced, whereas changes in the proportion widowed may relate to improving mortality in the population as a whole.

In 1994–95 the GHS was changed to allow same-sex couples to be identified, but this is only if they voluntarily identify themselves as members of a same-sex couple. Nevertheless, there has been a small increase in the proportion of individuals in same-sex couples since 1994–95.[14]

Marriage

Marriage rates have been declining, particularly at younger ages, since the 1970s.[22] The first marriage rate measures the number of single men and single woman marrying per 1,000 of the single population aged 16 and over. In 1971 the rates for England and Wales were 82.3 for males and 97.0 for females. In 2004 they were 25.7 for males and 30.8 for females.[22] The general decline in marriage numbers is mainly owing to a decline in first marriage rates.

The number of remarriages in England and Wales has remained fairly constant since the early 1970s yet, at the same time, the remarriage rates have also decreased considerably since then. One of the remarriage rates measures the number of divorced men and women marrying per 1,000 divorced people aged 16 or over. In 1971 this was 227.3 for men and 134.0 for women while in 2004 the equivalent figure was 45.7 for men and 33.8 for women. Therefore, it appears that the stability in the number of remarriages is largely a result of the increasing population of divorced individuals. The increase in divorced individuals is partly attributable to the Divorce Reform Act 1969, which came into effect in England and Wales in 1971.

Although annual marriage figures give a good indication of changes that are taking place in society, they do not always illustrate the experiences of groups of individuals who have been born in the same generation. This is necessary to discover how many people are ever-married by a certain age. Individuals in the same generation share similar economic and social conditions. Consequently, differences between generations should be one the strongest indicators of major trends existing in society. Ideally, it would be best to follow a particular group of individuals over time using a Longitudinal Study (LS) such as the ONS LS or British Household Panel Study. It is also possible, however, to use pseudo cohort analysis as used in Figure 1.14 to examine how changes have affected different individuals born in the same year group.

Figure **1.15**

Percentage of individuals married at survey by age at survey and year of birth, 1946–1960

Great Britain

Percentages

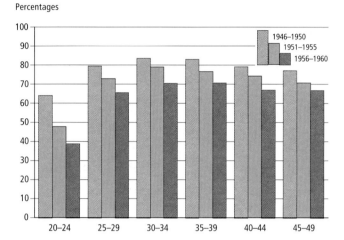

Source: GHS Time Series Dataset (1972–2004)

Figure **1.16**

Percentage of individuals divorced or separated (and not cohabiting) at survey by age at survey and year of birth, 1946–1960

Great Britain

Percentages

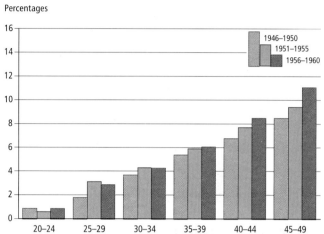

Source: GHS Time Series Dataset (1972–2004)

Figure 1.15 shows the percentage of men and women in Great Britain who were married at a particular age for three year groups. As well as confirming the general decrease in marriage (Figure 1.14), this figure shows that there has been a sharp decline in the proportion of individuals marrying aged 20 to 24. It also shows that the decrease is not caused entirely by a delay in marriage. If there was a delay in marriage for those born in 1956–60, then the proportion married at ages 45–49 would be similar to those born in earlier years. Of course, the figure does not show data for adults over 49 years old, but the most recent data does not show any evidence of a delay effect beyond this age.[23]

One problem with interpreting marriage trends occurs if there are large changes over time in the age gap between spouses. In part, this has been avoided in the above analysis by merging the data for males and females. However, it is also worth noting that age differences have been fairly stable in recent times. Although there is some debate about the distribution of age differences, in both 2001 and 1971 the mean age gap for all marriages was 2.6 years, with the average husband older than the average wife.[24, 25]

Divorce and separation

Figure 1.16 is similar to Figure 1.15 and shows the percentage of people in Great Britain who are separated or divorced (and not cohabiting) at the time of survey. Clearly, all individuals born in these three year groups have been affected by an increasing trend in marriage breakdown. Differences between the year groups demonstrate that the trend has more affect on younger generations, but the general trend is far more pronounced.

At younger ages separation is more prevalent than divorce. Taking an average of the three year groups, 1.5 per cent of individuals aged 20 to 24 years old were separated (and not cohabiting) at time of survey, compared with 0.8 per cent who were divorced. This difference can be explained by the fact that separation is often a precursor to divorce. Indeed, married or separated couples may not have been married for long enough to divorce. Since the Matrimonial and Family proceedings act was passed in 1984, couples can only divorce after completing 12 months of marriage (although previously this period was longer).

At older ages divorce is more prevalent than separation: 3.0 per cent of 45 to 49-year-olds were separated, compared with 9.6 per cent who were divorced. These proportions will be affected by the transition from marriage to separation, to divorce and then to remarriage. On average, it is likely that individuals spend less time in their lives being separated than they do being divorced. However, further research would be required to confirm this hypothesis.

Cohabitation

The proportion of cohabiting couple families has increased in recent years as more people choose to cohabit as a substitute for or precursor to marriage.[14] Marital status questions first included cohabitation as an option in the GHS in 1986. As such, there are no data available at early ages for the three year groups explored previously. Figure 1.17 shows the proportion of respondents in Great Britain who were cohabiting at the time of the survey. Data is only available for all three year groups at ages 35 years old and above.

Figure **1.17**

Percentage of individuals cohabiting at survey by year of birth and age at survey, 1946–1960

England and Wales

Percentages

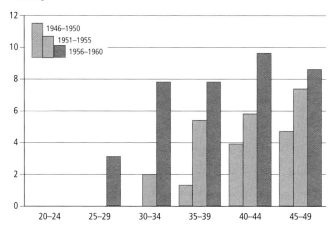

Source: GHS Time Series Dataset (1972–2004)

Figure **1.18**

Percentage of individuals cohabiting at survey by year of birth and age at survey, 1966–1980

England and Wales

Percentages

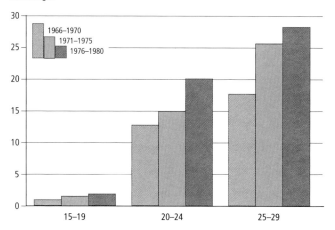

Note: Data are not yet complete for ages 25–29 where individuals were born from 1976–1980.

Source: GHS Time Series Dataset (1972–2004)

Between 1976 and 2004, the proportion of women aged 18 to 49 who were not married and were cohabiting trebled, from 9 per cent to 28 per cent. It is difficult to confirm exactly which demographic groups are responsible for this increase. Figure 1.17 suggests that it is partly related to marriage breakdown and remarriage as there is an increase in cohabitation after the average age of marriage. The rise in cohabitation above age 35 implies that cohabitation is not just a precursor to first marriage, but also a substitution for marriage or precursor to remarriage. The most recent GHS data for 2005 showed that 39 per cent of single individuals aged 25 to 34 were cohabiting. Although lower, this proportion for those aged 35 to 49 was 30 per cent. Similarly, the proportion of divorced men and women who were cohabiting was 47 per cent for those aged 25 to 34 and 41 per cent for those aged 35 to 49.[3]

Also of interest is that the proportion of individuals cohabiting becomes more stable for the most recent year group, those born 1956–60. This suggests that although cohabitation will continue to rise in the future, the rate of increase may slow. If each birth cohort reaches an 'equilibrium' level, then overall cohabitation rates will become more consistent in the future. This remains to be seen, but according to the 2003-based projections from the Government Actuary's Department, who have analysed recent trends, 'it has been assumed that proportions cohabiting will continue to increase for never-married people. But for other statuses, it has been assumed that proportions will remain constant at each age.[26]

Cohabitation prior to marriage has been a major influence both on the increase in cohabitation and the later age of marriage in recent decades.[14] Recent trends are difficult to demonstrate with certainty until a complete marital status history is available for birth cohorts (individuals grouped by year of birth). Nevertheless, Figure 1.18 shows the rise of cohabitation among individuals born between 1966 and 1980. Note that data are not yet complete for those born from 1976–1980 who are aged 25–29 years old.

It has been found that there is an increased risk of union breakdown among cohabiting couples compared with married couples.[27] From 1998 the GHS introduced a question on the number of past informal unions that did not lead to marriage, which allowed more analysis to be carried out on the relative stability of cohabiting unions compared to marriages. In 1998, 14 per cent of adults aged 16 to 59 reported at least one cohabiting union that did not lead to marriage; this proportion rose slightly to 16 per cent in 2004. Of this 16 per cent, three quarters had only one cohabiting union that did not lead to marriage, while one quarter had two or more.

Married and widowed adults were less likely than those of other marital statuses to report previous cohabiting unions that did not end in marriage. While 9 out of 10 adults had not lived in such a cohabiting union, nearly a third of divorced men and over a fifth of single and divorced women and single men had lived in at least one cohabiting union that did not lead to marriage.

Same-sex partnerships

There has been a small increase in the proportion of individuals in same-sex couples since same-sex couples could be recorded in responses to the GHS in 1994–95. However, same-sex cohabitation is only recorded if the information is volunteered by the survey respondent. As such, the proportion of individuals in same-sex partnerships may be underestimated by the GHS.

In December 2005 legislation introducing Civil Partnerships came into effect and provisional data are now available for the first Civil Partnerships that have occurred.[28] According to provisional figures, same-sex couples formed 18,059 civil partnerships in the UK between December 2005 and the end of December 2006. Of these, 16,173 took place in England with 1,131 in Scotland, 627 in Wales and 128 in Northern Ireland.

Notes and References

1   Allan G and Crow G (2001) *Families, Households and Society.* Palgrave Macmillan: Basingstoke.

2   Haskey J (1996) 'Population review: Families and households in Great Britain', *Population Trends* 85 pp 7–24.

3   Office for National Statistics (2006) General Household Survey 2005, ONS: Newport, available at: www.statistics.gov.uk/StatBase/Product.asp?vlnk=5756

4   Berthoud R and Gershuny J (2000) Seven years in the lives of families: Evidence on the dynamics of social change from the British Household Panel Survey, The Policy Press: Bristol.

5   Office for National Statistics (2007) *Social Trends 37,* Palgrave Macmillan: Basingstoke, available at: www.statistics.gov.uk/socialtrends37/

6   Office of the Deputy Prime Minister (2003). *Housing and Households: 2001 Census and other Sources,* HMSO: London.

7   Household and population estimates and projections, available at: www.communities.gov.uk/index.asp?id=1156093

8   Office for National Statistics (1997) Social Focus on Families, TSO: London.

9   Murphy M (1997) 'Changes in living arrangements in Britain in the last quarter century: insights from the General Household Survey', in Rowlands O, Singleton N, Maher J and Higgins V, *Living in Britain*, ONS, TSO: London, pp 179–190, available at: www.statistics.gov.uk/downloads/theme_compendia/GHS_1995_v1.pdf

10 Haskey J (1994) 'Stepfamilies and stepchildren in Great Britain', *Population Trends* 76 pp 17–28.

11 Data for 1971 and 1972 are from the GHS and are not available for Northern Ireland, 2005 data are for the UK and derived from the LFS.

12 Chamberlain J, Gill B (2005) 'Chapter 5: Fertility and mortality', in Office for National Statistics, *Focus on People and Migration*, Palgrave Macmillan: Basingstoke, pp 71–90, available at:

www.statistics.gov.uk/statbase/Product.asp?vlnk=12899. For the latest (2006) TFR see: www.statistics.gov.uk/cci/nugget.asp?ID=951

13 Haskey J (1995) 'Trends in marriages and cohabitation: the decline in marriage and the changing pattern of living in a partnership', *Population Trends* 80, pp 5–15.

14 Haskey J (2001) 'Cohabitation in Great Britain: past, present and future trends – and attitudes', *Population Trends* 103, p 4–25, available at:www.statistics.gov.uk/downloads/theme_population/PT103book_v3.pdf.

15 *Focus on Ethnicity and Identity*, available at: www.statistics.gov.uk/cci/nugget.asp?id=458

16 Office for National Statistics (2006) *Focus on Ethnicity and Religion*, Table 4.4, Palgrave Macmillan: Basingstoke, available at: www.statistics.gov.uk/StatBase/Product.asp?vlnk=14629

17 Office for National Statistics (2005) *Focus on Older People*, Palgrave Macmillan: Basingstoke, available at: www.statistics.gov.uk/focuson/olderpeople/

18 Evandrou M (2000) 'Social inequalities in later life: the socioeconomic position of older people from ethnic minority groups in Britain', *Population Trends* 101, pp 32–39, available at: www.statistics.gov.uk/cci/article.asp?ID=556&Pos=2&ColRank=1&Rank=64

19 Office for National Statistics (2005) *Focus on People and Migration*, Palgrave Macmillan: Basingstoke, available at: www.statistics.gov.uk/statbase/Product.asp?vlnk=12899

20 Adoptions by date of entry into the adopted children register, these data are only available from 1996 for the UK. Adoptions by date of court order are not available for the UK. Adopted children are included in the definition of families used in this report. Foster children are not included in families as they are not related to their foster parents. Data on adoptions in England and Wales are available in series FM2, available at: www.statistics.gov.uk/statbase/Product.asp?rlink=581

21 Much of this section has been prepared using the GHS Time Series Dataset (1972–2004), available to download from ESDS at: www.esds.ac.uk/findingData/ghsTitles.asp

Pseudo-cohort analysis represents the average experiences of people belonging to a particular cohort, and does not track the experiences of actual people. It is not possible to determine the duration of a particular event. For example, it is not possible to know how long a person has been married. In essence, the experiences of different individuals are compared as opposed to the same individuals (true cohort analysis). The GHS started in 1971 and has been carried out continuously since then, except for breaks in 1997–1998 when the survey was reviewed and 1999–2000 when the survey was redeveloped. Following the 1997 review, the survey was re-launched from April 2000 with a different design. The GHS began reporting on a financial-year basis from 1988, instead of a calendar year, and data are published annually. In addition, since 1994 the GHS has been conducted using face to face computer-assisted personal interviewing (CAPI), with some self-completion. Because of its history and changes to the survey over time, GHS data does not represent a perfect time series and should be interpreted with caution.

22 Data on marriage and divorce are available from ONS in the *Series FM2* and *Population Trends* publications, available at: www.statistics.gov.uk/statbase/Product.asp?vlnk=581 www.statistics.gov.uk/StatBase/Product.asp?vlnk=6303

23 Marriages in 2005 (provisional), selected data tables, England and Wales, available at: http://nswebcopy/statbase/Product.asp?vlnk=1 4275&More=n

24 Bhrolchain MN (2005) 'The age difference at marriage in England and Wales: a century of patterns and trends', *Population Trends* 120, pp 7–14. http://nswebcopy/cci/article.asp?ID=1232&Pos=1&C olRank=1&Rank=224

25 Hancock, R, Stuchbury, R and Tomassini, C (2003) 'Changes in the distribution of marital age differences in England and Wales, 1963 to 1998', *Population Trends* 114, pp 19–25.

26 GAD cohabitation assumptions for the 2003-based population projections, available at: www.gad.gov.uk/marital_status_projections/2003/ cohabitation_assumptions.htm

27 Haskey J (1999) 'Cohabitational and marital histories of adults in Great Britain', *Population Trends* 96, pp 13–24.

28 Civil Partnerships – selected data tables (provisional), available at: http://nswebcopy/statbase/Product.asp?vlnk=14675

Unpaid care and the family

Linda Pickard

Chapter 2

Introduction

Unpaid family care has been given a great deal of emphasis in social care policy in the UK in the last two decades. This has been primarily associated with policies emphasising care in the community, since these policies place much reliance on unpaid care and support provided by family members. The emphasis on unpaid care has also arisen in the context of the growing numbers of older people, many of whom rely exclusively on their families for support.

The 2001 Census was the first to collect information on the provision of unpaid care in the population. The census data provide an opportunity to re-examine provision of unpaid care in this country, since they allow for analyses of care provision by important sub-groups of the population. Of particular interest are those who are cohabiting and those in different minority ethnic groups, on whom research has previously been restricted by small numbers in sample surveys. In some respects, however, the census data on unpaid care are limited in scope, since they only cover whether, and for how long per week, care is provided. There is no information in the census on whom care is provided for or whether care is provided on a co-resident or extra-resident basis.

Because of the limitations of census data, this chapter includes 2000/01 GHS data on provision of unpaid care by a sample of the adult population living in private (non-institutional) households in Great Britain. The GHS data on provision of informal care provide much more detail than is contained in the census data, albeit relating to a sample of the population. Moreover, as this chapter will show, by analysing the family type of carers using the census data and supplementing this with insights gained from the GHS data, the census can be used to examine key aspects of unpaid care and the family. This includes care provided by older people for their spouses and intergenerational care provided by mid-life people for their parents.

This chapter is particularly concerned with unpaid care and the family. Although the census does not allow us to look at who is being cared for, other sources enable us to look specifically at unpaid family care. Unpaid family care is defined as both the provision of care within the family unit and the provision of care to extended family. Like the GHS, the analysis of 2001 Census data on unpaid care focuses on **provision of unpaid care by adults living in private households**. Adults are defined here as people aged 19 and over (see Glossary). The chapter begins with an overview of numbers of carers and their characteristics. It then looks at provision of care by legal and *de facto* (actual) marital status, family type and ethnicity, before discussing a number of key issues in relation to unpaid care and the family in the UK today.

Numbers and characteristics of people providing unpaid care

Numbers and types of unpaid carers

In 2001 there were approximately 5.5 million adults aged 19 and over in Great Britain providing unpaid care, constituting approximately 13 per cent of the population living in private households. In the census, people providing unpaid care include those who look after family, friends or neighbours who are in need of help because of illness, disability or old age (see Appendix for the census question on unpaid care).

The proportion of the population providing unpaid care in the 2001 Census appears to be lower than estimates derived from the 2000/01 GHS, which found that 16 per cent of the adult population in households provided informal care.[1] This difference in the proportions of the population providing unpaid care is partly explained by a difference in the definitions of caring. The GHS asks about all informal care, whereas the census asks about care provided for one hour a week or more. The census therefore excludes people providing very small amounts of care (see Appendix).

A smaller proportion of the population provides intense unpaid care. These 'heavy duty' carers are usually defined in terms of long hours of caring, often providing care for 20 hours a week or more. Heavy duty caring is particularly important because of its impact on the carer and because it is more likely to act as a substitute for formal services. In this case, the results from the 2001 Census and the 2000/01 GHS are similar. Both the census and the 2000/01 GHS show approximately 4 per cent of the adult population providing unpaid care for 20 hours a week or more in Great Britain (see Appendix), representing approximately 1.8 million adults.

The majority of unpaid care is family care. Table 2.1 shows that at least 70 per cent of all informal carers provide care to relatives, including parents and parents-in-law, spouses and children. The remaining 30 per cent provide care to other family members, friends or neighbours. The correspondence between unpaid care and family care is even greater for longer hours of care. Of all care provided for 20 hours a week or more, over 90 per cent is provided to relatives, particularly partners and parents.

Unpaid care is not necessarily provided on a co-resident basis and more often is provided on an extra-resident basis. Table 2.2 shows that about a third of carers are caring for someone living with them and two-thirds are caring for someone living elsewhere. However, the locus of care does vary by the intensity of caring. Three quarters of those caring for 20 hours a week or more are caring for someone living in the same household as themselves.

Table 2.1

Provision of unpaid care by adults[1]: by relationship of care-recipient to carer and hours of care, 2000/01

Great Britain   Percentages

Care recipient:	All care	Care for 20 hours a week or more
Spouse/partner	19	46
Child (any age)	7	15
Parent/parent-in-law	44	31
Other relative or friend	30	8
Weighted base (000's) = 100%	6,585	1,755
Unweighted sample	2,273	605

1 People aged 19 and over in households (see Appendix).

Source: 2000/01 GHS (author's analysis)

Table 2.2

Provision of unpaid care by adults[1]: by locus of care and hours of care 2000/01

Great Britain   Percentages

	All care	Care for 20 hours a week or more
Carer's household	32	75
Other private household only	68	25
Weighted base (000's) = 100%	6,585	1,755
Unweighted sample	2,273	605

1 People aged 19 and over in households.

Source: 2000/01 GHS (author's analysis)

Characteristics of unpaid carers

Unpaid care varies by gender and age. Of the 5.5 million adults who provided unpaid care in Great Britain in 2001, the majority (58 per cent) were women: approximately 3.2 million women and 2.3 million men provided unpaid care for an hour a week or more. Of those providing unpaid care for long hours, over 60 per cent were women. There were over a million women and nearly three quarters of a million men providing unpaid care for 20 hours a week or more in Great Britain in 2001.

The peak ages for provision of care are in mid-life. Figure 2.3 shows that in 2001 over one in five of the population aged 51 to 59 were providing unpaid care for an hour a week or more. By comparison, Figure 2.4 shows that intense care (20 hours a week or more) was provided most often by adults in mid-life and older. Between the ages of 56 and 74, over 6 per cent of the population were providing care for 20 hours a week or more.

Figure 2.3

Percentage of adults[1] who provide care for one or more hour(s) per week: by age, 2001

Great Britain

Percentages

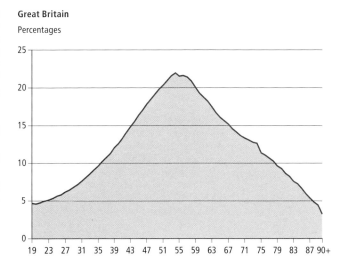

1 People aged 19 and over in households.

Source: 2001 Census, Office for National Statistics; General Register Office for Scotland

Figure 2.4

Percentage of adults[1] who provide care for twenty hour(s) per week or more: by age, 2001

Great Britain

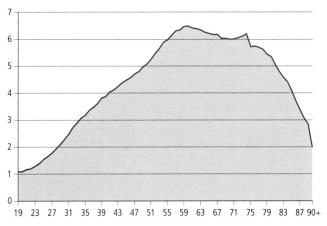

1 People aged 19 and over in households.

Source: 2001 Census, Office for National Statistics; General Register Office for Scotland

The balance of care provision between women and men also varies by age. Although women predominate in the provision of care in most age groups, gender differences are particularly marked in mid-life. Figure 2.5 shows the percentage of adult women and men who provide care for one hour or more every week by age. Between the ages of 30 and 59, there are approximately 5 per cent more women than men providing care for one hour a week or more. For adults aged 70 and over, the general trend is reversed, and the proportion providing care is higher for men than women.

Marital and cohabitation status and provision of unpaid care

In this volume, a family is generally defined as a married or cohabiting couple with or without child(ren), or a lone parent with child(ren) (see Glossary). As noted elsewhere in the volume, the majority of families in the UK are married or cohabiting couple families. As with other topics in family demography, a key issue in looking at the provision of unpaid care within families is whether there are differences between married and cohabiting couples. Before looking at the family type of carers, it is therefore useful to begin by looking at the impact of *de jure* (legal) and *de facto* (actual) marital status on the provision of unpaid care.

Legal marital status and provision of unpaid care

The marital status, age and gender of unpaid carers are shown in Table 2.6. Generally, those who are married are more likely to provide unpaid care than those who are single or previously married. This is the case for both men and women and across all age groups. Among adults who were married in 2001, 16 per cent provided care for one hour or more a week. This compares with 8 per cent of single adults and 10 per cent of previously married adults. There are similar patterns in provision of intense forms of care (Table 2.7).[2] Approximately 6 per cent of married adults provided care for 20 hours a week or more, compared with 2 per cent of single adults and 3 per cent of previously married adults.

Although married people are more likely to provide care overall, there are variations from the overall pattern by age and gender. Under the age of 30, previously married adults have similar rates for the provision of unpaid care to married adults. For adults aged 30 to 44, the figures for married and previously married adults are also similar. However, for adults aged 45 and over, there are clear differences between married adults and previously married adults. These differences are even more evident for adults aged 65 and over. The proportion of single adults providing care is lower than the proportion of married adults for almost all age groups. The exception is adults aged 45 to 64, where a slightly larger proportion of single men provide care for 20 hours a week or more than either married or previously married men. Single people in mid-life and previously married people aged under 45 will include those caring for parents and some lone mothers caring for sick or disabled children.[3]

Figure **2.5**

Percentage of adults[1] who provide care for one or more hour(s) per week: by gender and ten-year age bands, 2001

Great Britain

Percentages

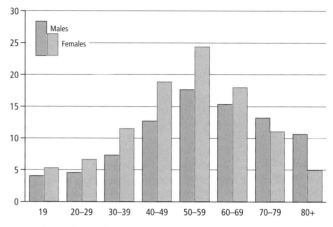

1 People aged 19 and over in households.

Source: 2001 Census, Office for National Statistics; General Register Office for Scotland

Table **2.6**

Percentage of adults[1] who provide care for one or more hour(s) per week: by legal marital status, gender and age, 2001

Great Britain

Percentages

Gender and marital status	Age				
	<30	30–44	45–64	65+	Total
Men					
Married	6	9	18	16	14
Single	4	8	16	8	7
Widowed/divorced/ separated	6	8	11	6	8
Total	5	9	16	13	11
Women					
Married	9	14	24	18	19
Single	6	11	22	9	9
Widowed/divorced/ separated	9	13	17	5	10
Total	7	13	23	11	14
Men and women					
Married	8	12	21	17	16
Single	5	9	18	9	8
Widowed/ divorced/separated	8	11	15	5	10
Total	6	11	20	12	13

1 People aged 19 and over in households.

Source: 2001 Census, Office for National Statistics; General Register Office for Scotland

Table **2.7**

Percentage of adults[1] who provide care for twenty or more hour(s) per week: by legal marital status, gender and age, 2001

Great Britain   Percentages

Gender and marital status	Age				
	<30	30–44	45–64	65+	Total
Men					
Married	2	3	4	8	5
Single	1	2	6	3	2
Widowed/divorced/ separated	2	2	3	2	2
Total	1	2	4	6	3
Women					
Married	3	5	8	10	7
Single	1	4	8	3	3
Widowed/divorced/ separated	4	5	5	1	3
Total	2	4	7	5	5
Men and women					
Married	3	4	6	9	6
Single	1	3	7	3	2
Widowed/divorced/ separated	3	4	4	2	3
Total	2	3	6	6	4

1. People aged 19 and over in households.

Source: 2001 Census, Office for National Statistics; General Register Office for Scotland

De facto marital status and provision of unpaid care

The 2001 Census offers the first opportunity to explore the relationship between cohabitation and unpaid caring. As suggested at the beginning of the chapter, the sample sizes of cohabiting carers are too small in household surveys like the GHS to allow for detailed examination of cohabitation and caring. Yet this is important because it is not clear that relationships based on cohabitation imply the same obligations and ties as those based on legal marriage. This may have consequences where the provision of care is concerned, especially between partners/spouses.[4] As one author recently observed:

> Given that cohabitation has a higher likelihood of ending in separation as opposed to legal marriage... it may be argued that late-life alliances cannot provide the same stability or cross-kin interactions and relationships as those supported or created by marriage-based families or stepfamilies. This may have consequences in later life with regard to reciprocal care.[5]

Overall, the 2001 Census suggests that provision of care by adults in cohabiting couples is lower than provision of care by adults in married couples. Whereas 16 per cent of people in married couples provide care for one hour a week or more, only 9 per cent of people in cohabiting couples do so. Figure 2.8 shows that a smaller proportion of cohabiting adults provide care at all ages. Similarly, with regard to intense forms of care, approximately 6 per cent of people in married couples provide care for 20 hours a week or more, as opposed to 3 per cent of those in cohabiting couples. Again, Figure 2.9 shows that a

Figure **2.8**

Percentage of adults[1] who provide care for one or more hour(s) per week: by partnership status and 5-year age bands, 2001

Great Britain

Percentages

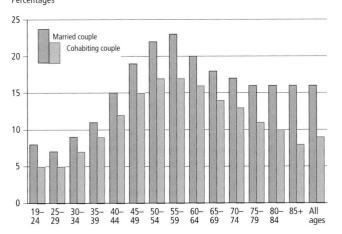

1 People aged 19 and over in households.

Source: 2001 Census, Office for National Statistics; General Register Office for Scotland

Figure **2.9**

Percentage of adults[1] who provide care for twenty or more hour(s) per week: by partnership status and 5-year age bands, 2001

Great Britain

Percentages

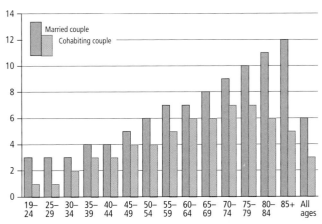

1 People aged 19 and over in households.

Source: 2001 Census, Office for National Statistics; General Register Office for Scotland

smaller proportion of cohabiting adults provide care at all ages, in this case for 20 hours per week or more.

Considering Figures 8 and 9 together, the differences between married and cohabiting couples are particularly striking with regard to people in mid-life and in older age groups. At ages 55 to 59, for example, while 23 per cent of people in married couples provide care for an hour a week or more, only 17 per cent of those in cohabiting couples do so. Indeed, with regard to the provision of care for 20 hours a week or more by older people, the trends by age for people in married and cohabiting couples seem to diverge. Whereas for married people, the probability of providing care in the older age groups increases with age, for those in cohabiting couples, the probability of providing care declines from the age of 70 onwards.

Figure 2.10 shows the proportion of adults providing intense care according to a combination of partnership and marital status. It examines whether the provision of unpaid care by people who are cohabiting is more similar to provision of care by people who are married or people who are neither married nor cohabiting. (The figure shows care provided for 20 hours a week or more, although care provided at lower levels of intensity reveals similar patterns.)

Under the age of 45, cohabiting adults are more similar to single (never married) non-cohabiting adults than to adults who are married or adults who were previously married and are not cohabiting. Between the ages of 45 and 64, the proportion of cohabiting adults providing intense care remains lower than the proportion of married adults providing this form of care. For these ages, it is also lower than the proportion of single adults not cohabiting (which includes lone parents who have never married). For adults aged 65 and over, cohabiting adults have a higher proportion providing intense care than both single and previously married adults who are not cohabiting.

Overall, cohabiting adults do not seem to provide unpaid care at a similar level to other groups, married or otherwise. While the proportions are very similar for cohabiting and single adults (not cohabiting) up to the age of 44, they are very different for those aged 45 and over. Considering all this, it seems important to retain a distinction between married and cohabiting couples when looking at provision of care.

The family type of carers

Married and cohabiting couple families

Consistent with the analysis so far, the probability of providing unpaid care is higher, controlling for age, in married couple families than in cohabiting couple families. This is true both where care is provided for one hour a week or more and where care is provided for 20 hours a week or more (Table 2.11).

Figure 2.10

Percentage of adults[1] who provide care for twenty or more hour(s) per week: by partnership status, legal marital status of those not in couples and age bands, 2001

Great Britain

Percentages

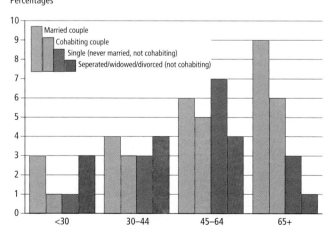

Note: Figure 2.9 illustrates the proportions for married and cohabiting couples in more detail.
1 People aged 19 and over in households.

Source: 2001 Census, Office for National Statistics; General Register Office for Scotland; Individual SAR from the 2001 Census (for those not living as couples)

Table 2.11

Percentage of adults[1] who provide care for twenty or more hour(s) per week: by family type and age, 2001

United Kingdom

Percentages

Family type and hours of care provided per week (p.w.)	Age				
	<30	30–44	45–64	65+	All
One or more hour(s) p.w.					
Married couple family	6	12	21	17	16
Cohabiting couple family	5	9	16	12	9
Lone parent family	9	15	23	11	15
Not in family	4	8	12	5	7
All	6	11	20	12	13
Twenty or more hours p.w.					
Married couple family	2	4	6	9	5
Cohabiting couple family	1	3	5	6	3
Lone parent family	3	6	11	7	7
Not in family	1	1	2	1	1
All	2	4	6	6	4

1 People aged 19 and over in households

Source: Individual SAR from the 2001 Census

As shown in Chapter One, the majority of people live in married couple families. Similarly, the majority of people providing unpaid care live in married couple families – this type of family accounts for nearly three-quarters of all people providing care for an hour a week or more according to the 2001 Census (Figure 2.12). In contrast, a much smaller proportion live in cohabiting couples: less than 10 per cent of all people providing care for one hour or more per week. The concentration of carers in married couple families is particularly marked where long hours of care are

Figure **2.12**

Family type of adults¹ providing care for one or more hour(s) a week: by age bands, 2001

United Kingdom
Percentages

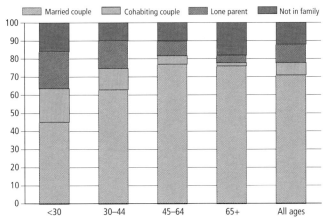

1 People aged 19 and over in households.
Source: Individual SAR from the 2001 Census

Figure **2.13**

Family type of adults¹ providing care for twenty hours a week or more: by age band, 2001

United Kingdom
Percentages

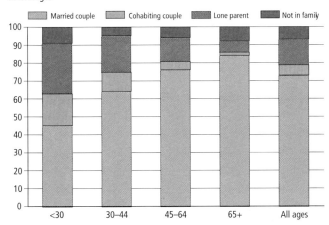

1 People aged 19 and over in households.
Source: Individual SAR from the 2001 Census

provided at older ages. For people aged 65 and over, 84 per cent of people providing care for 20 hours a week or more are in married couple families (Figure 2.13).

The distribution of people providing care between families containing married and cohabiting couples partly reflects the greater likelihood observed above (Figures 2.8 and 2.9), that people who are married will provide care compared to people who are cohabiting.

However, the distribution of married and cohabiting adults providing care primarily reflects the greater prevalence of married couple families in the population, especially in the age groups where care-giving is greatest. As already noted, the probability of providing care is generally highest among people in mid-life and in older age groups (Figures 2.3 and 2.4), yet it is in these age groups that the probability of being in a cohabiting couple family is currently lowest.[6] As noted in Chapter One, cohabiting couple families are the youngest families, with half of all cohabiting couple families in the UK headed by a person aged under 35 in 2001. Although the probability of providing care tends to be lower in cohabiting couple families than in married couple families (Table 2.11), cohabiting couple families make up only a small proportion of families in mid-life and older age groups. Therefore cohabitation is unlikely to have much impact on provision of care at present. However, the impact of cohabitation on caring may be greater in future years, an issue that will be discussed more fully at the end of this chapter.

Married couple families with and without children

People in married couple families who provide care are evenly divided between families with and without children (Figure 2.14). However, there are variations with the age of the carer and intensity of care provided, in part reflecting the predominant ages at which couples have dependent children in the household. In younger age groups, carers are more likely to be in married couple families with children; in mid-life, carers in married couple families are approximately evenly divided between families with and without children. At older age groups, carers are most likely to be in married couple families without children. Indeed, provision of care by people aged 65 and over is dominated by one family type, married couple families without children.

Around two-thirds of people providing care for one hour a week or more who are aged 65 and over are in married couple families without children (Figure 2.14). The proportion is even higher for people providing care for long hours. Nearly three-quarters of people aged 65 and over who are providing care for 20 hours a week or more are in married couple families without children (Figure 2.15).

Figure **2.14**

Family type of adults¹ providing care for one or more hour(s) a week: by presence of children in family and by age band, 2001

United Kingdom

Percentages

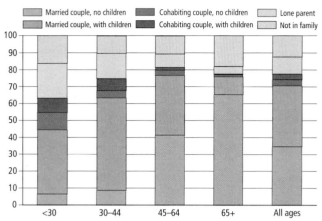

1 People aged 19 and over in households.

Source: Individual SAR from the 2001 Census

Figure **2.15**

Family type of adults¹ providing care for twenty or more hours a week: by presence of children in family and by age band, 2001

United Kingdom

Percentages

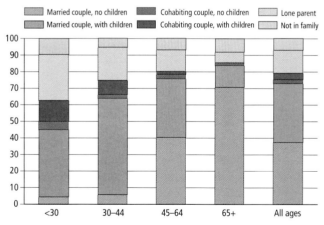

1 People aged 19 and over in households.

Source: Individual SAR from the 2001 Census

Older people and spouse care

Care provided for long hours by people living in married couple families without children tends to be 'spouse care', which is care for a husband or wife. The 2000/01 GHS data suggest that nearly three-quarters of all care for 20 hours a week or more provided by people living in married couples without children is provided to a spouse or partner (Table 2.16). The

tendency of intense carers living in married couples without children to provide care to a spouse increases with age. For people aged 65 and over living in married couples without children, nearly 90 per cent of care (provided for 20 hours a week or more) is provided to a spouse.

The census shows that there are approximately 350,000 people aged 65 and over living in married couples without children who are providing care for 20 hours a week or more. If the same proportion is providing care to a spouse as in the GHS sample, then this implies that there are nearly a third of a million people aged 65 and over providing care for 20 hours a week or more to a spouse in this type of family alone. Since most older people are married to people in approximately the same age group as themselves, this demonstrates the extent to which older people themselves contribute towards the care of other older people. This confirms what has been recognised in recent years as 'the volume of care provided by spouses, most of whom are themselves elderly'.[7, 8]

Provision of long hours of care in older married couple families (without children) is almost equally divided between women and men. However, as Figure 2.17 shows, it does vary according to age. Between the ages of 65 and 74, women outnumber men in provision of care for long hours, but at ages 75 and over men outnumber women. Of the total number of people aged 65 and over providing care for 20 hours a week or more in married couple families without children, approximately 175,000 are men and 170,000 are women. Gender equality is widely recognised as a characteristic of provision of care for spouses in older age groups. As one study put it, 'spouse care by elderly people breaks normal gender boundaries of caring'.[9] However, the provision of intense unpaid care to spouses by older people does have implications for the health of carers, which are explored later in this chapter.

Lone parent families and co-resident care for parents

At almost all ages, people living in lone parent families are more likely than those in other family types to be providing care (Table 2.11). This is true for both care provided for one hour a week or more and care provided for twenty hours a week or more. The only exception is that for ages 65 and over, adults in married couple families are more likely to provide care. Comparing the summary figures, those living in lone parent families have only a slightly lower overall probability of providing care for an hour or more than those living in married couple families (15 per cent in lone parent families compared with 16 per cent in married couple families). Indeed, those living in lone parent families are more likely to be providing care for 20 hours a week or more than are those in married

Table **2.16**

Provision of care for twenty hours a week or more by adults[1]: by family type, relationship of care recipient to carer and age band, 2000/01

Great Britain   Percentages

Family type and age-band	Spouse	Child	Parent	Other	Weighted sample base (thousands) = 100%)	Unweighted sample
Under 65						
Married couple, no children	56	6	32	5	360	134
Married couple, with children	35	25	36	4	517	169
Lone parent	2	32	63	3	178	60
Under 65 total	34	19	40	7	1,250	425
65 and over						
Married couple, no children	89	-	8	3	403	147
Married couple, with children[2]	[55]	[36]	[9]	[-]	24	7
Lone parent[2]	-	[73]	[12]	[15]	26	8
65 and over total	74	7	9	11	505	180
All ages						
Married couple, no children	73	3	20	4	763	281
Married couple, with children	36	26	35	4	547	176
Lone parent	1	37	57	5	204	68
All ages total	45	15	31	8	1,765	605

Note: Cohabiting couple families are not identified separately because the sample sizes are too small for analysis.
1 People aged 19 and over in households.
2 Percentages are shown in square brackets where the underlying sample base (unweighted sample row total) is less than 50.

Source: 2000/01 GHS (author's analysis)

Figure **2.17**

Provision of care for twenty hours a week or more by people[1] aged 65 and over in married couple families without children: by gender and age band, 2001

Great Britain
Thousands

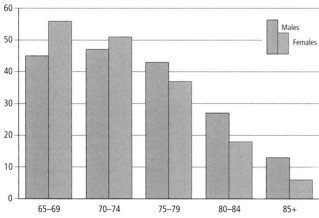

1 People in households.

Source: 2001 Census, Office for National Statistics; General Register Office for Scotland

couple families (7 per cent in lone parent families compared to 5 per cent in married couple families).

Figure 2.18 shows that adults in lone parent families are more likely to provide unpaid care between the ages of 45 and 64 than at any other age. More than one in ten people aged 45 to 64 living in lone parent families provide care for 20 hours a week or more. Moreover, the probability of providing care in this age group is somewhat higher for men living in lone parent families than for women (13 per cent for men and 11 per cent for women).

Adult carers living in lone parent families primarily provide care to sick, disabled and elderly parents and to sick and disabled children (Table 2.16). For adults in lone parent families providing care for 20 hours a week or more, the GHS sample suggests that the majority are providing care to parents. In other words, care provided by adults in lone parent families is primarily care provided by adult 'children' in the family for their parents. The literature on informal care suggests that men constitute a relatively high proportion of unmarried children caring for

Figure **2.18**

Percentage of adults[1] who provide unpaid care for twenty hours a week or more in lone parent families: by gender and age band, 2001

United Kingdom

Percentages

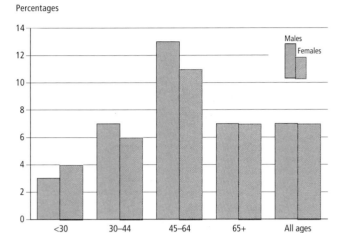

1 People aged 19 and over in households.

Source: Individual SAR from the 2001 Census

widowed parents, usually in the parent's own home.[10] This may be because British men leave the parental home at a later age than women, and are less likely to leave the parental home at all.[11]

Although the probability of providing care in lone parent families is high, adults providing care in lone parent families constitute a relatively small proportion of all adults providing care. Approximately one in ten adult carers providing care for an hour a week or more live in lone parent families, with a slightly higher proportion for care provision of 20 hours a week or more (Figures 2.12 and 2.13).

Lone parent families are, however, not the only family type where adults provide long hours of unpaid care to their parents. Where the carer is under the age of 65, the GHS data shows that a considerable proportion of adults caring for 20 hours a week or more in married couple families are providing care to parents (Table 2.16). Such care is likely to be provided both within the immediate family on a co-resident basis and on an extra-resident basis to a parent living in another household. Intergenerational care for parents is considered further in the next section.

Older people not in a family and intergenerational care

The overwhelming majority of people in the UK live in a family, as defined in this volume (see Chapter 1 and Glossary). This is not the case, however, for some sub-groups of the population, particularly very old people who are important to consider in the context of unpaid care. Figure 2.19 shows the proportion

Figure **2.19**

Family type of people[1] aged 65 and over: by age band, 2001

United Kingdom

Percentages

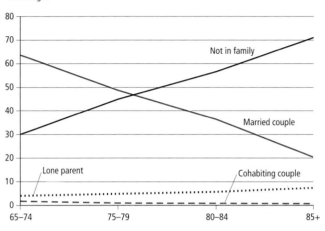

1 People in households.

Source: Individual SAR from the 2001 Census

Figure **2.20**

Family type of people[1] aged 85 and over by provision of unpaid care and hours of care provided, 2001

United Kingdom

Percentages

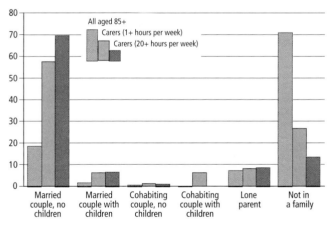

1 People in households.

Source: Individual SAR from the 2001 Census

of people aged 65 and over living in different family types by age band, and includes those not in a family. The chart shows that the proportion of people living in a family decreases after the age of 65 and that by the age of 75, the majority of older people do not live in a family. Indeed, nearly three-quarters of people aged 85 and over are in this position. Although some people who do not live in a family share a household with others, almost two-thirds (64 per cent) of people aged 85 and over in private households live alone.[12] This is important because it is among the 'oldest old' that care needs are greatest.

As noted earlier, care provision by people in older age groups is concentrated in married couple families (Figures 2.14 and 2.15). Additionally, when provided for long hours, the care recipient is most commonly a spouse (Figure 2.16). However, the proportion of adults in married couple families declines as old age progresses (Figure 2.19). By the time people are aged 85 and over, 70 per cent of care for 20 hours a week or more is provided by individuals in a married couple family (without children), but 70 per cent of people in this age group do not live in a family at all (Figure 2.20).

Therefore, after the age of 75 the majority of people do not receive care from their spouses. For these older people, help from the succeeding generation is more important than spouse care.[13] Data from the 2002/03 English Longitudinal Study of Ageing (ELSA) show that, for people aged 75 and over with a functional disability, the most important sources of help are often children (Table 2.21).[14] More disabled people aged 75 and over receive help from a daughter than from a spouse. For people aged 75 and over, intergenerational care is the single most important source of unpaid care for those in need of help.

The age gap between older parents in receipt of care and children providing care is, on average, approximately thirty years.[15] Therefore, people aged 75 and over receiving help from the succeeding generation are likely to receive care from people who are in mid-life. The figures at the beginning of this chapter showed that the likelihood of providing care is greatest for adults in mid-life, and a major reason for this is provision of care to older parents and parents-in-law. The GHS sample shows that people providing care in mid-life are more likely to provide help to a parent or parent-in-law than to anyone else

(Figure 2.22). Moreover, where care is provided for long hours, parents are the largest single group of beneficiaries of care provided by carers under the age of 65 (Table 2.16).

The majority of people providing care in mid-life are women. Indeed, the disparity in care provision between women and men is greater between the ages of 45 and 64 than at any other age band.[16] Around three quarters of people providing

Figure **2.22**

Provision of unpaid care by adults aged 16[1] and over: by relationship of care-recipient to carer, 5-year age bands, 2000/01

Great Britain

Percentages

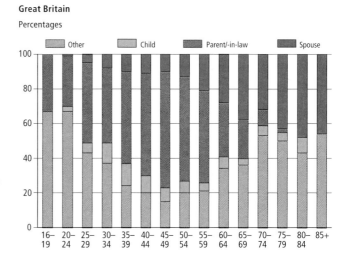

1 People in households.

Source: 2000/01 GHS (author's analysis)

Figure **2.23**

Provision of unpaid care for twenty hours a week or more by married adults[1]: gender and 5-year age bands, 2001

Great Britain

Thousands

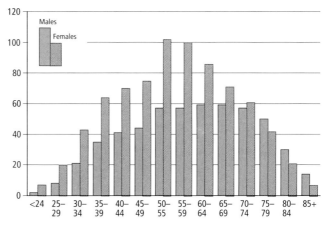

1 People aged 19 and over in households.

Source: 2001 Census, Office for National Statistics; General Register Office for Scotland

Table **2.21**

Reported source of help for people with a functional disability, aged 60 and over: age band, 2002/03

England

		Percentages
Source of help:	60–74	75+
No help	64	46
Spouse or partner	23	16
Parent	<1	<1
Daughter	9	17
Son	6	11
Daughter/son-in-law	3	7
Sibling	2	2
Grandchild	5	5
Other unpaid	11	11
Other paid	16	16
Sample	2,759	1,942

Source: English Longitudinal Study of Ageing (ELSA), 2002/03

care, whether for one hour or more a week or 20 hours or more, live in married couple families (Figures 2.12 and 2.13) and the majority are married women. Figure 2.23 shows the large disparity in provision of care for 20 hours a week or more between married women and married men in mid-life. There are approximately 200,000 married women in their 50s providing care for 20 hours a week or more, compared to just over 100,000 married men. Provision of care for long hours is, therefore, at its greatest for married women when they are of working age (that is, below state pension age). The provision of intense care by married women of working age has implications for their economic activity, an issue examined in more detail later in the chapter.

Minority ethnic groups and the provision of unpaid care

The 2001 Census is particularly important for information on unpaid care provision by people from different ethnic groups. Before the 2001 Census, research on unpaid care provided by people from different ethnic groups was restricted by small numbers in sample surveys. Ethnic group differences in provision of care, however, are particularly important in the present context because they are likely to be partly related to variations in family composition.

Census data show that in 2001 there are approximately 320,000 adults from minority ethnic groups providing unpaid care for one hour a week or more in England and Wales (Table 2.24). Of these, approximately a third provide unpaid care for 20 hours a week or more. Approximately half of all carers from minority ethnic backgrounds are from Indian or Pakistani backgrounds. Without carrying out a separate

analysis, it appears that the number of carers from different minority ethnic groups generally reflects the underlying size of the minority ethnic populations.[17]

The majority of adults providing unpaid care from minority ethnic backgrounds are women, although this varies considerably by ethnic group and hours of care provided. Approximately 70 per cent of Pakistani and Bangladeshi adults providing unpaid care for 20 hours a week or more are women, compared to just over half of Indian adults providing care for one hour a week or more.

It is particularly important to take age into account when looking at provision of care by different ethnic groups because differences in age structure between ethnic groups are likely to affect the probability of providing care. Figure 2.25 shows the proportion of adults providing care for one hour a week or more by age group for ethnic groups with the largest numbers of carers. The figure shows that adults under 30 from all minority ethnic groups are more likely than people from White backgrounds to provide care. However, at mid-life (ages 45 to 64) people from White backgrounds are more likely than those from any other ethnic background to provide care. These differences in provision of care between ethnic groups over the life course may reflect the fact that minority ethnic populations are younger than the White population and are therefore less likely to have frail older family members in need of care.[18]

Nevertheless, where long hours of care are provided, people from some minority ethnic backgrounds are more likely to provide care than people from White backgrounds, irrespective of age. In particular, people from Asian or Asian British backgrounds are more likely to provide care for 20 hours a

Table **2.24**

Provision of unpaid care by adults[1]: by ethnic group, hours of unpaid care and gender, 2001

England and Wales

Thousands

Hours of unpaid care per week and gender	White	Indian	Pakistani	Bangladeshi	Caribbean	Black Black African	Other minority ethnic groups[2]	All minority ethnic groups
One or more hours per week								
Men	1,974	46	25	9	16	10	32	138
Women	2,723	52	34	12	26	14	43	182
All	4,698	98	60	21	42	24	75	320
Twenty or more hours per week								
Men	599	14	9	3	5	4	11	46
Women	903	22	19	7	8	6	17	79
All	1,501	36	28	10	13	10	28	125

1 People aged 19 and over in households.
2 Other minority ethnic groups include Mixed; any other Asian background; any other Black background; and Chinese or other ethnic group.

Source: 2001 Census, Office for National Statistics

Figure **2.25**

Percentage of adults[1] who provide unpaid care for one hour a week or more: by ethnic group and age band, 2001

England and Wales

Percentages

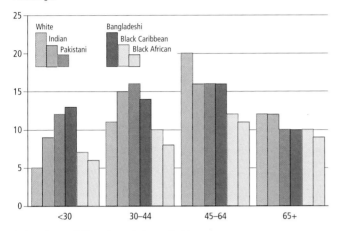

1 People aged 19 and over in households.

Source: 2001 Census, Office for National Statistics

week or more compared to those from all other ethnic backgrounds at all ages, although the differences are particularly marked at younger age groups (Figure 2.26). Pakistani and Bangladeshi adults aged under 30 are five times more likely than people from White backgrounds to provide care for 20 hours a week or more. Between 45 and 64 years old, people from Bangladeshi backgrounds are nearly twice as likely to provide long hours of care than their White counterparts.

Figure **2.26**

Percentage of adults[1] who provide unpaid care for twenty hours a week or more: by ethnic group and age band, 2001

England and Wales

Percentages

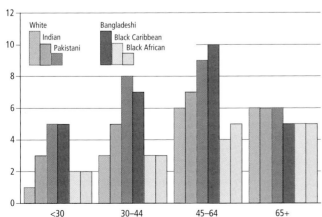

1 People aged 19 and over in households.

Source: 2001 Census, Office for National Statistics

These ethnic group differences in provision of care for long hours, which have also been observed elsewhere in analyses using the 2001 Census,[19, 20] are likely to be related to differences in family and household structure. Extended multigenerational households are a common feature of South Asian communities,[21] and this type of household has been associated with provision of long hours of intergenerational care.[22]

The family type of carers varies with ethnic group. Figure 2.27 shows the family type and ethnic group of adults providing care for 20 hours or more per week. A much greater proportion of intense unpaid care is provided by people from minority ethnic groups in families with children. This includes couple families with children and lone parent families. By comparison, there is a much greater proportion of intense unpaid care provided by couples with no children from White backgrounds than other ethnic groups. This reflects the greater tendency for families headed by a person of non-White ethnic background to have children living with them, compared with White families.[23]

Provision of care by people from minority ethnic backgrounds is undergoing considerable change. Minority ethnic populations are ageing,[24] yet at the same time factors such as the increasing participation of minority ethnic women in the labour market are placing strains on family support systems.[25] Issues around provision of unpaid care and economic activity in the population as a whole are discussed further in the next section.

Figure **2.27**

Family type of adults[1] providing unpaid care for twenty hours a week or more: by ethnic group[2], 2001

England and Wales

Percentages

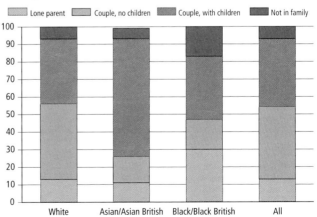

1 People aged 19 and over in households.
2 Asian or Asian British backgrounds include Indian, Pakistani, Bangladeshi and any other Asian background; Black or Black British backgrounds include Caribbean, African and any other Black background.

Source: Individual SAR from the 2001 Census

Issues in the provision of unpaid care and the family

The health of unpaid carers

There has been considerable debate in the research literature as to whether caring has a damaging effect on the health of carers. While evidence is somewhat inconclusive, it suggests that the physical health of carers and non-carers is similar once age and gender are taken into account.[26] There is greater evidence that caring can negatively affect the psychological health of carers, however, and a large international literature suggests that this may be particularly acute for carers of older people with dementia.[27]

The 2001 Census shows that one in four of all carers themselves have health problems, as indicated by self-reported limiting long-term illness. The proportion is higher where care is provided for long hours, and among carers providing care for 20 hours a week or more, one in three report having a limiting long-term illness. The proportion reporting health problems is particularly high among older carers who spend long hours caring. Over half (55 per cent) of people aged 65 and over providing care for 20 hours a week or more report a limiting long-term illness, which could be physical or psychological (Figure 2.28). This is somewhat higher than the corresponding proportion among people of this age in the general population (50 per cent).

It is therefore clear that the majority of older carers, many of whom are spouse carers, have health problems and may themselves be in need of help and support. The numbers of spouse carers is expected to increase in future years,[28] raising

questions about the extent to which the future care of older people may come to depend increasingly on people who are themselves in poor health.

Provision of unpaid care and economic activity

The majority of people who provide unpaid care are of working age, below the current state pension age (60 for women, 65 for men). The 2001 Census shows that there are over four million people of working age providing care for at least one hour a week (Figure 2.29) and, of these, 1.2 million people provide care for 20 hours a week or more (Figure 2.30). The majority of people of working age who provide care are women; nearly three-quarters of a million provide care for 20 hours a week or more. Women thus comprise 60 per cent of those of working age who provide long hours of care.

Long hours of care are not generally compatible with full-time employment:[29] nearly three-quarters (70 per cent) of all working age people providing care for 20 hours a week or more do not work full time. The 2001 Census shows that there are over three-quarters of a million people of working age providing care for 20 hours a week or more who are either economically inactive or who work part time. Of these, 70 per cent are women (Figure 2.30).

The relationship between caring and employment does not necessarily imply that it is the long hours of care that lead people to withdraw, either wholly or partially, from the labour market. People who provide care may be those who are

Figure **2.28**

Percentage of adults[1] with a limiting long-term illness: by age band and hours of caring, 2001

United Kingdom
Percentages

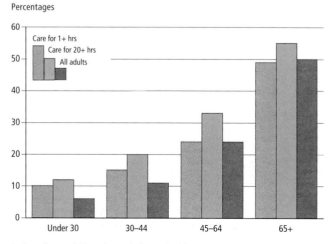

1 People aged 19 and over in households.

Source: Individual SAR from the 2001 Census

Figure **2.29**

Provision of unpaid care for one hour a week or more by adults below state retirement age[1]: by gender and economic activity, 2001

Great Britain
Thousands

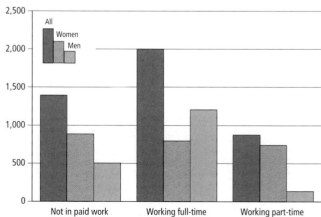

1 Adults in households below state retirement age refer to women aged between 16 and 59 and men aged between 16 and 64.

Source: 2001 Census, Office for National Statistics; General Register Office for Scotland

already out, or partially out, of the labour market. It is likely that caring and employment interact, influencing each other in both directions, depending on the intensity of the care provided, the characteristics of the carer and the nature of the caring relationship.[30]

Issues around employment and unpaid care are of rising importance nationally. The employment rates of women are rising, and women are the main providers of unpaid care at working age.[31] At the same time, there is increasing demand for care, as the numbers of older people, particularly the very old, continue to rise. There is therefore increasing pressure on people, especially women, both to provide unpaid care to family members and to participate in the paid labour market.

Carers who provide long hours of care while being in paid employment can experience considerable stress.[32] Alternatively, those who give up or reduce paid work may suffer financial consequences, including lower incomes, diminished career prospects, and reduced occupational and personal pensions.[33] In the longer term, there are concerns that rising employment rates among women, in particular, may affect the provision of unpaid family care in the future.

Changing family forms and the future of unpaid care

The future provision of unpaid care is likely to be affected by a number of aspects of change in marriage and fertility patterns, such as the changing nature of relationships, smaller family

sizes and rising childlessness.[34] For the first time, the 2001 Census has allowed an exploration of the relationship between one of these areas, cohabitation, and the provision of unpaid care. Cohabiting relationships cover a wide range of levels of commitment – while some are a precursor or substitute for marriage, others are more transitory. The census suggests that provision of care by adults in cohabiting couples is lower than provision of care by adults in married couples. However, the impact of cohabitation on numbers of people providing care is relatively small at present because cohabitation is concentrated in younger age groups, where care provision is at its lowest.

In future years it is projected that the numbers of people who are cohabiting in the age groups where care provision is concentrated, mid-life and older age groups, will increase markedly.[35] The latest official marital status projections for England and Wales show that between 2003 and 2031 there will be an increase of nearly 250 per cent in numbers of people aged 45 to 64 who are cohabiting, and an increase of over 450 per cent in numbers of people aged 65 and over who are cohabiting (Figure 2.31). People who are cohabiting will represent nearly one in three of all mid-life people in marital and cohabiting unions by 2031, compared to less than 10 per cent at present. There are projected to be approximately half a million people cohabiting aged 65 and over by 2031, although these will still form less than 10 per cent of all older people in marital and cohabiting unions.

The implication is that cohabitation may have a greater impact on provision of care in future, initially in relation to provision of care by people in mid-life, and in the longer term in relation to

Figure **2.30**

Provision of unpaid care for twenty hours a week or more by adults below state retirement age[1]: by gender and economic activity, 2001

Great Britain

Thousands

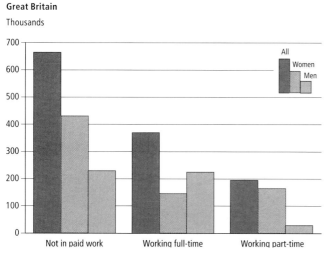

1 Adults in households below state retirement age refer to women aged between 16 and 59 and men aged between 16 and 64.

Source: 2001 Census, Office for National Statistics; General Register Office for Scotland

Figure **2.31**

Cohabiting population aged 16 and over by age, 2002–2031

England and Wales

Thousands

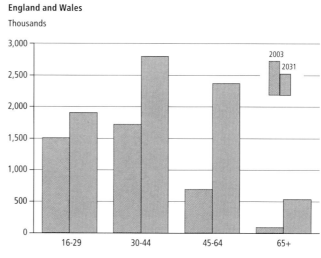

Source: 2003-based GAD projections (www.gad.gov.uk)

provision of care in older age groups. However, as cohabitation in mid-life and older age groups becomes more general, the impact of cohabitation on provision of care in future will in part depend on whether there is any convergence in the behaviour of cohabiting and married couple families with regard to the provision of unpaid care.

Notes and references

1   Office for National Statistics (2002) *Carers 2000*, TSO: London, p 2, available at:
www.statistics.gov.uk/downloads/theme_health/carers2000.pdf

2   Further information on the characteristics of carers is available from Office for National Statistics (2006) 'Chapter 12: Caring and carers' in *Focus on Health*, Palgrave Macmillan: Basingstoke, available at: www.statistics.gov.uk/focuson/health/

3   Office for National Statistics (2002) as above, p 4.

4   Clarke L (1995) 'Family care and changing family structure: bad news for the elderly?', in Allen I and Perkins E (eds) *The Future Of Family Care For Older People*, HMSO: London, p 34.

5   Harper S (2004) 'The challenge for families of demographic ageing', in Harper S (ed) *Families in Ageing Societies: A Multi-Disciplinary Approach*, Oxford University Press: Oxford, p 22.

6   Office for National Statistics (2006) General Household Survey 2005, Table 5.4, available at:
www.statistics.gov.uk/downloads/theme_compendia/GHS05/marriage&cohabfinal.xls

7   Arber S and Ginn J (1991) *Gender and Later Life: A Sociological Analysis of Resources and Constraints*, Sage: London, p 136.

8   Clarke L (1995) as above, p 24.

9   Arber S and Ginn J (1991) as above, pp 135–6.

10 Arber S and Ginn J (1991) as above, p 137

11 Parker G (1993) 'Informal care of older people in Great Britain: the 1985 General Household Survey', in Twigg J (ed) *Informal Care in Europe*, Social Policy Research Unit: University of York, p 156.

12 Office for National Statistics (2003) *People Aged 65 and Over*, TSO: London, p 7

13 Pickard L, Wittenberg R, Comas-Herrera A, King D, Malley J (2007) 'Care by spouses, care by children – Projections of informal care for older people in England to 2031', *Social Policy & Society* 6, pp 353–366.

14 The following reference offers further discussion relating to this section: Marmot M, Banks J, Blundell R, Lessof C and Nazroo J (eds) (2003) *Health, Wealth and Lifestyles of the Older Population in England: the 2002 English Longitudinal Study of Ageing*, Institute for Fiscal Studies: London.

15 Hirst M (1999) *Informal Care-Giving in the Life-Course*, Social Policy Research Unit (SPRU): University of York, p 34.

16 Office for National Statistics (2002) as above, p 4.

17 Office for National Statistics (2005) 'The UK population: past, present and future', in *Focus on People and Migration*, Palgrave Macmillan: Basingstoke, pp 13–14.

18 Evandrou M (2005) 'Health and social care', in Office for National Statistics, *Focus on Older People*, Palgrave Macmillan: Basingstoke, p 64.

19 Evandrou M (2005) as above, p 64.

20 Young H, Grundy E and Kalogirou S (2005) 'Who cares? Geographic variation in unpaid caregiving in England and Wales: evidence from the 2001 Census', *Population Trends* 120, p 32.

21 Katbamna S, Ahmad W, Bhakta P, Baker R and Parker G (2004) 'Do they look after their own? Informal support for South Asian carers', *Health and Social Care in the Community* 12 (5), p 402.

22 Pickard L (2002) 'The decline of intensive intergenerational care of older people in Great Britain', 1985–1995, *Population Trends* 110, pp 31–41.

23 See the previous *Focus on Families* work on ethnicity, available at: www.statistics.gov.uk/CCI/nugget.asp?ID=1167

24 Evandrou M (2000) 'Ethnic inequalities in health in later life', *Health Statistics Quarterly* 8, p 20.

25 Katbamna *et al* (2004) as above, p 399.

26 Parker G and Lawton D (1994) *Different Types of Care, Different Types of Carer: Evidence From The General Household Survey*, HMSO: London, pp 43–47.

27 Bauld L, Chesterman J, Davies B, Judge K and Mangalore R (2000) *Caring for Older People: An Assessment of Community Care in the 1990s*, Ashgate Publishing Ltd: Aldershot, p 104.

28 Pickard L, Wittenberg R, Comas-Herrera A, Davies B and Darton R (2000) 'Relying on informal care in the new century? Informal care for elderly people in England to 2031', *Ageing and Society* 20, pp 745–772.

29 Joshi H (1995) 'The labour market and unpaid caring: conflict and compromise', in Allen I and Perkins E (eds) *The Future of Family Care for Older People*, HMSO: London, p 93–118.

30 Evandrou M (1995) 'Employment and care, paid and unpaid work: the socio-economic position of informal carers in Britain', in Phillips J (ed) *Working Carers*, Avebury Publishing Ltd: Aldershot.

31 Mooney A and Statham J with Simon A (2002) *The Pivot Generation. Informal Care and Work After Fifty*, The Policy Press: Bristol.

32 Arksey H (2002) 'Combining informal care and work: supporting carers in the workplace', *Health and Social Care in the Community* 10 (3), p 152.

33 Evandrou M and Glaser K (2003) 'Combining work and family life: the pension penalty of caring',. *Ageing and Society* 23, pp 583–601.

34 Clarke L (1995) as above, pp 19–49.

35 Population projections are available at: www.gad.gov.uk

Family structure and family formation – education as outcome and explanation

Richard Lampard

Chapter 3

Introduction

Previous studies have shown parental divorce, or living in a lone parent family in childhood, to have an impact on educational attainment. Educational attainment has also been shown to have an impact on age at marriage and the proportion marrying. This chapter uses data from census tabulations, relating to highest level of qualifications and also to student status, to examine the relationship between family type and educational outcomes, and the relationship between education and first marriage. The chapter also refers to the findings of previous research, which act as a point of comparison for the census results.

Much of the existing research on these relationships in the UK has made use of a small number of longitudinal studies. Findings from such studies are liable to sampling error and the effects of sample attrition, and may not be representative of the general population. They are also specific to particular birth cohorts.

The analyses of census data in this chapter also focus on specific cohorts, but complete coverage allows the educational attainments of individuals of a specific age to be examined accurately and without any sampling-related biases. The 2001 Census also collected more detailed information relating to education than any previous census, as well as collecting extensive information on family relationships. While research based on census data has its own limitations, it nevertheless complements research based on other data sources.

PART ONE: Family type and educational outcomes

Couples, parents and qualifications

An overall picture of the educational qualifications of adults within families is provided by Table 3.1. The educational qualifications correspond to the Family Reference Person and their partners (except for lone parents). The percentage of adults in married couple families with no children who have no academic or professional qualifications is much higher than that for married couple families with dependent children. Conversely, the equivalent percentage for cohabiting couple families with no children is lower than that for cohabiting couple families with dependent children. Of course, these results

Table **3.1**

Highest level of qualification of Family Reference Person and partners according to family type and presence or absence of dependent/non-dependent children, 2001

Great Britain

Percentages

		Base	No academic or professional qualifications	Level 1/2	Level 3	Level 4/5	Other qualifications/ level unknown	Not applicable
Adults in lone parent families	Dependent children	1,788,500	30.0	44.7	6.7	13.6	4.3	0.6
	Non-dependent children only	834,949	40.8	16.4	2.8	9.2	5.7	25.0
	Total	2,623,449	33.5	35.7	5.5	12.2	4.8	8.4
Adults in married couple families	No children	10,785,050	36.5	20.9	4.5	16.7	8.3	13.1
	Dependent children	8,799,632	17.7	43.8	7.9	25.2	5.3	0.1
	Non-dependent children only	3,048,102	43.5	24.3	4.2	12.8	11.4	3.8
	Total	22,632,784	30.1	30.3	5.8	19.5	7.6	6.8
Adults in cohabiting couple families	No children	2,553,340	14.9	37.3	11.6	30.4	4.3	1.5
	Dependent children	1,608,646	22.0	50.3	7.6	14.8	5.1	0.2
	Non-dependent children only	166,654	40.8	30.7	4.9	11.9	9.9	1.8
	Total	4,328,640	18.5	41.9	9.9	23.9	4.8	1.0
Total adults in families	No children	13,338,390	32.3	24.1	5.9	19.3	7.5	10.9
	Dependent children	12,196,778	20.1	44.8	7.7	22.1	5.1	0.2
	Non-dependent children only	4,049,705	42.9	22.9	3.9	12.0	10.2	8.1
	Total	29,584,873	28.7	32.5	6.4	19.5	6.9	6.1

Note: Not applicable contains all families where the Family Reference Person is aged 75 or over.
     The numbers presented here may differ from other census outputs because of changes relating to disclosure and confidentiality.

Source: 2001 Census, Office for National Statistics; General Register Office for Scotland

may reflect the age distributions of adults within different family types because, for example, many of the married couples with no children in their households are older couples.

The percentages of adults in families with non-dependent children only who have no academic or professional qualifications are higher than the equivalent percentages for families with dependent children. Again this result may reflect the age distributions of adults within different family types, since parents will tend to be older in families in which children are non-dependent rather than dependent. The highest percentages corresponding to Level 4 or 5 qualifications are for adults in cohabiting couple families with no children and married couple families with dependent children. These results, and for that matter the other results, may also reflect relationships between educational attainment, parenthood, and age at marriage.[1]

Educational outcomes among 17-year-olds

Previous longitudinal studies have shown parental divorce, or living in a lone parent family in childhood, to have an impact on educational attainment.[2] Such studies, however, have often also shown that when other factors such as financial difficulties are taken into account, the impact of parental divorce or absence is reduced, and in some instances becomes statistically insignificant.[3] While a cross-sectional source cannot provide the same scope as longitudinal studies for examining the relationship between family histories and educational outcomes, the 2001 Census nevertheless provides scope for examining the relationship between current family or household characteristics and the educational characteristics of resident children.

Figure **3.2**

Total number and proportion of single individuals who are not lone parents, are aged 17, and are living within families, by family type, 2001

Great Britain

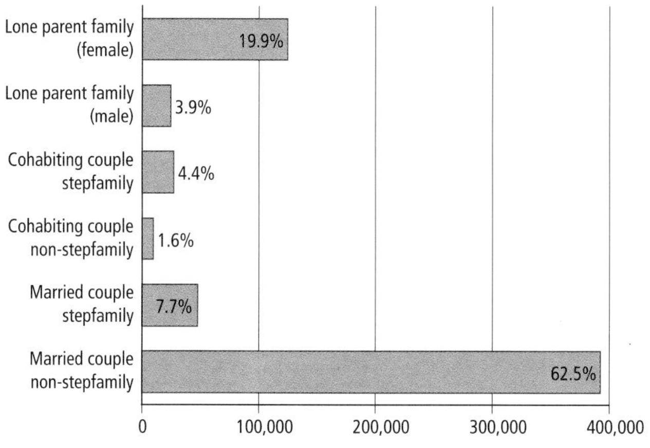

Source: 2001 Census, Office for National Statistics; General Register Office for Scotland

For many 16-year-olds at the census date, full-time education was still obligatory and there had not yet been an opportunity to acquire educational qualifications. However, as age increases beyond 16, the likelihood of children having left their parental homes increases. Reasons for leaving home may be linked to educational achievement, such as entry into higher education, or, conversely, to a lack of educational achievement. Hence this analysis focuses on 17-year-olds. The 17-year-old cohort possessed a degree of diversity at the census date in terms of educational outcomes, but was still predominantly living within families with a parent or parents. Figure 3.2 shows the total number of children aged 17 included in this analysis for each family type.

The analysis excludes 17-year-olds who were not living in their parental homes at the census date, as well as those who were students away from home at term-time addresses. It also excludes 17-year-olds who were living within their parental homes, but were also living with a spouse or cohabiting partner, or as a lone parent.[4] According to the census, in 2001 in Great Britain 89.7 per cent of 17-year-olds were single and living in families with a parent or parents. Of the remainder, 2.0 per cent were married or living with a partner, 0.7 per cent were lone parents, and 7.5 per cent were not living in a family unit. The majority (54.6 per cent) of those excluded from the analysis were female.

In this part of the chapter, educational outcomes are represented by two measures: being in full-time education at age 17 and highest level of qualifications at age 17.

Children in education

Figure 3.3a and Table 3.3b show, for each sex, the percentage of 17-year-olds in Great Britain[5] in full-time education according to family type. Note that 57.3 per cent of 17-year-olds not living within families were in full-time education, with the figure for married or cohabiting 17-year-olds being 20.0 per cent, and the figure for 17-year-old lone parents being 13.5 per cent.[6]

The variations by family type in Table 3.3b are similar for each sex, although the percentages corresponding to male children vary slightly more than those corresponding to female children. This may reflect the proportion of male children who are not in full-time education being higher for every family type. For all family types, there are more female children in full-time education than male children. (A more detailed analysis of gender differences is carried out later in the chapter – see Figure 3.8).

Married couple non-stepfamilies have the highest percentage of 17-year-olds in education. The next highest percentage, which corresponds to female lone parent families, is substantially lower, 10.4 percentage points lower for male children and 8.6 percentage points lower for female children. However, while differences are clearly evident, the validity and

Figure **3.3a** and Table **3.3b**

Single individuals who are not lone parents, are aged 17, and are living within families by family type and sex: percentages in full-time education, 2001

Great Britain — Percentages

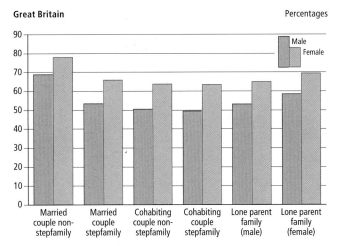

Source: 2001 Census, Office for National Statistics; General Register Office for Scotland

Great Britain — Percentages

	Male	Female
Married couple non-stepfamily	68.9	77.9
Married couple stepfamily	53.5	65.8
Cohabiting couple non-stepfamily	50.6	63.7
Cohabiting couple stepfamily	49.5	63.4
Lone parent family (male)	53.2	64.9
Lone parent family (female)	58.5	69.3

Note: For base numbers see Appendix, Table A4.

reliability of any conclusions drawn from such results must be reflected upon carefully (see Box 1).

The percentages of children aged 17 in full-time education for all other family types are discernibly lower than those for married couple non-stepfamilies and female lone parent families. The lowest percentages are for cohabiting couple families and do not differ markedly between cohabiting couple stepfamilies and non-stepfamilies. An examination of the data in Table 3.3b sub-divided between England, Wales and Scotland showed the difference between female lone parent families and the four family types with lower percentages to be less marked in Wales and Scotland than it was in England.[7]

The relationship between family type and being in full-time education (Table 3.3b) may in part reflect a relationship between family type and the ages at which children leave home. For example, at the time of the census, 19.9 per cent of all 17-year-olds in Great Britain who lived with a parent or parents lived in female lone parent families. However, the equivalent figure for 16-year-olds was 21.2 per cent.[6] This decline with increasing age suggests that children living in female lone parent families may be more likely to leave home or live away from home at an earlier age.

Table 3.4 shows the percentages of children aged 16, 17 and 18 living with a parent or parents in each family type. The percentage corresponding to married couple non-stepfamilies increases with age, a movement opposite to the trend for female lone parent families. One possible explanation is that there are different rates of leaving home for children in different family types. If leaving home is associated with not being in full-time education, this will have an impact on the percentage in full-time education corresponding to children still living in families.

Table **3.4**

Family type by age for children living with a parent or parents, 2001

Great Britain — Percentages

	Age 16	Age 17	Age 18
Married couple non-stepfamily	60.5	62.5	63.6
Married couple stepfamily	7.9	7.7	7.7
Cohabiting couple non-stepfamily	1.8	1.6	1.5
Cohabiting couple stepfamily	4.7	4.4	4.3
Lone parent family (male)	3.8	3.9	4.1
Lone parent family (female)	21.2	19.9	18.8

Source: 2001 Census, Office for National Statistics; General Register Office for Scotland

Differential rates of leaving home between family types would result in this effect varying in magnitude. Furthermore, any association between not being in full-time education and leaving home may vary according to family type. For example, children in female lone parent families may be more likely to leave home if they do not remain in education.[8]

Qualifications

Being in full-time education at age 17 has potential implications for an individual's future prospects and level of qualifications. The census gathers information on levels of qualifications for each household member[9] and in the 2001 Census, just over 87 per cent of all 17-year-olds in England and Wales possessed qualifications at Level 1 or higher. Level 1 corresponds to one of the following:

- one or more 'O' level passes
- one or more CSEs/GCSEs at any grade
- NVQ level 1
- Foundation level GNVQ.[10]

Box 1

Interpretations of apparent differences in educational outcomes between the various family types need to acknowledge several factors:

The difference between correlation and causation

Higher proportions of children in full-time education may be associated with married couple families, but this does not mean that parents' marital status causes a greater proportion of children to attend school or college. For example, it may be that such differences in educational status between family types are caused by another factor, such as household income.

Results from the census are a snapshot in time

The census only reports a child's family type at the time the census was taken. It does not report the length of time that the child has been in its current family type or the family type(s) experienced previously. Children aged 17 may have experienced a number of different family forms during their childhood and the family types that they belong to at the census date do not reveal this. For example, the children belonging to lone parent families do not include those who spent some of their childhood in a lone parent family after parental separation, but whose lone parent subsequently re-partnered. Since re-partnering rates vary according to a

range of characteristics, 17-year-olds living with lone parents cannot justifiably be viewed as representative of all 17-year-olds who have ever experienced life in a lone parent family.

Methodology

The results presented in the first section of this chapter only examine the educational situations of 17-year-olds of each sex in relation to family types and the NSSEC categories of their households. (NSSEC stands for National Statistics Socio-Economic Classification, a system defined in more detail later in this chapter). A more sophisticated analysis would control for other factors that may affect educational attainment.

Response issues

Although the census has the advantage of covering the whole population, some of the data are nevertheless imputed.[11] There are also likely to be differences between self-reported information (census) and information collected by interviews. A comparison of 2001 Census data and Labour Force Survey (LFS) market indicators showed that:

- for most categories of employed people, the LFS estimated a higher proportion of individuals with high level qualifications
- for those who were unemployed or economically inactive, the opposite was the case, with the LFS estimating a lower proportion with high qualifications[11]

For Level 2 or higher, the figure was just over 65 per cent. Level 2 corresponds to five or more GCSEs at grades A–C, or some equivalent.[6] Thus, not only does Level 2 correspond to a standard benchmark of achievement at age 16, it also provides a reasonable degree of variability as an educational outcome for comparisons between different family types or between other groups.

For each sex, Table 3.5 shows the percentage of 17-year-olds in England and Wales with qualifications at Level 2 or higher according to family type. In comparison, note that 54.6 per cent of 17-year-olds not living within families possessed qualifications at Level 2 or higher, whereas the figure for married or cohabiting 17-year-olds was 42.2 per cent and the figure for 17-year-old lone parents was 25.0 per cent.[6]

As for full-time education, the highest percentage with qualifications at Level 2 or higher corresponds to married couple non-stepfamilies. The difference in percentage points between the family types with the highest and second highest percentages can be examined: for full-time education, this difference is 10.4 for male children and 8.6 for female children. For qualifications, the equivalent differences are 14.6 and 12.1.

Table **3.5**

Qualifications at Level 2 or higher for individuals aged 17: by family type and sex, 2001

England and Wales   Percentages

| | Qualifications at Level 2 or higher | | | |
| | Male | | Female | |
	Percentage	Base	Percentage	Base
Married couple non-stepfamily	67.8	*185,273*	77.7	*171,456*
Married couple stepfamily	53.2	*23,425*	65.6	*21,404*
Cohabiting couple non-stepfamily	47.0	*4,939*	59.7	*4,320*
Cohabiting couple stepfamily	50.6	*13,417*	64.3	*12,088*
Lone parent family (male)	50.4	*13,072*	64.2	*9,570*
Lone parent family (female)	51.2	*57,021*	63.3	*55,758*

1 30 cases that were not allocated to an appropriate family type have been excluded from consideration.

Source: 2001 Census, Office for National Statistics

In other words, married couple non-stepfamilies differ more from other families with respect to qualifications.

The family type with the second highest percentage of children with qualifications at Level 2 or higher is married couple stepfamilies. So, while female lone parent families have, by a clear margin, the second highest percentage of children in full-time education, this is not necessarily accompanied by Level 2 or higher qualifications.

The lowest percentages are for cohabiting couple non-stepfamilies, with only 47.0 per cent of male children having qualifications at Level 2 or higher, compared with 67.8 per cent for married couple non-stepfamilies. Thus, in terms of children having qualifications at Level 2 or higher, the difference between cohabiting couple non-stepfamilies and married couple non-stepfamilies is greater than the difference between married couple stepfamilies and married couple non-stepfamilies. Interestingly, the differences between male and female lone parent families in the percentages in full-time education are not apparent for the percentages with qualifications at Level 2 or higher. An examination of the data in Table 3.5 sub-divided between England and Wales again shows that, in Wales as compared to England, 17-year-olds living in female lone parent families had performed less well relative to those living within other family types.[7]

Findings from previous studies

Relationships between family type and educational outcomes have been found in earlier academic studies, although these studies have varied conclusions. One study carried out research based on two longitudinal studies, the National Child Development Survey (NCDS) and the British Cohort Study (BCS), and focused on individuals born in Great Britain in 1958 and 1970. It showed parental divorce by age 16 to be associated with a lack of academic or vocational qualifications in adulthood. This effect became smaller in magnitude, but nevertheless persisted, when account was taken of a range of socio-economic and other factors.[2]

This was reinforced by another study that analysed NCDS data and found that living in a lone parent family in childhood had a negative impact on educational attainment by age 23, even for those who did not experience financial difficulties. This was not true, however, for the relationship between ever having been in a lone parent family and staying on at school at age 16, which was not statistically significant once the existence of financial difficulties had been taken into account.[12]

Other studies have found that taking account of socio-economic factors, such as financial difficulties, reduces the impact of parental divorce or parental absence so that it is no longer statistically significant. One study, examining NCDS data, focused on the attainment of 'A' levels and higher qualifications and did not find a significant impact corresponding to the absence of a parent (of either sex) at age 16 once financial difficulties had been controlled for.[3]

A further study, again using NCDS data, focused on parental divorce between ages 9 and 16. It found that the overall impact on the likelihood of obtaining any qualifications was reduced considerably, and became statistically insignificant, when various factors measured at age 7, including financial hardship, were taken into account.

However, this study also found that parental divorce between ages 9 and 16 did seem to have an impact on male children's attainment of higher level qualifications.[13] This was statistically significant even after controlling for the factors measured at age 7. Research using data from the Youth Cohort Study of England and Wales (YCS) do not concur with this, however. In this study, coming from a lone parent family did not have a statistically significant impact on young people's likelihood of entry into higher education after controlling for various individual and family characteristics.[14]

Other studies, though, have found that the effects of living in a lone parent family in childhood persist when socio-economic factors are taken into account. Research using data from the British Household Panel Survey (BHPS) has shown that the likelihood of attaining A level (or higher) qualifications was lower for individuals born between 1970 and 1983 when they had experienced a non-intact (lone parent) family before age 16.[15]

This finding was most marked where there was experience of a lone parent family at an age of younger than six, after controlling for various family background characteristics, including parents' educational levels. The difference also persisted when family background characteristics were taken into account in a fuller fashion via the use of sibling data.[16] Another piece of research using the BHPS found that the negative effect of ever living in a lone parent family on educational attainment persisted when attention was restricted to poorer families.[17]

Stepfamilies

Children in Education

As suggested in Box 1, generalisations about particular family types should be treated with caution. This is partly due to the variety of family compositions that are contained within each family type. Stepfamilies constitute a good example of this. The children living in a stepfamily may be the biological or adopted children of one or both partners. The relationships between children in stepfamilies including more than one child are also varied. The point in a child's life when they start living in a stepfamily varies, and cannot be established from the census. Table 3.6 represents an attempt to investigate one aspect of the complexity of stepfamilies, and shows the educational status of 17-year-olds in stepfamilies according to whether or not they are stepchildren. It is evident that a substantial majority of 17-year-olds in married couple stepfamilies are stepchildren.

Both the results for stepchildren and those for non-stepchildren vary according to sex. This variation is broadly in line with the general pattern, with 9 to 15 per cent more female children in full-time education than male children. Furthermore, the difference between stepchildren and non-stepchildren within stepfamilies is not the same for the two sexes. There is a slightly lower percentage of male stepchildren in full-time education when compared with male non-stepchildren, both for married and cohabiting couple stepfamilies.

For female children, the difference is less clear. Female stepchildren in cohabiting couple stepfamilies exhibit the same pattern as male children: a slightly lower percentage in full-time education than non-stepchildren. However, female stepchildren in married couple stepfamilies are marginally more likely to be in full-time education than their non-stepchildren counterparts.

Caution should be exercised when interpreting these differences, as the census presents only a snapshot of the family on the census date and the family history is not recorded. The results for 17-year-olds living in stepfamilies who are not stepchildren relate only to children who were living with a stepsibling, stepsiblings or half sibling(s) at the census date. Those 17-year-old non-stepchildren who had previously lived with one or more stepsiblings or half siblings, but whose stepsiblings or half siblings had left home before the census date, will have been classified as living in a non-stepfamily rather than a stepfamily. This reflects the cross-sectional nature of the census.

Additionally, not all stepchildren in cohabiting couple stepfamilies appear to have been identified as such. Stepfamilies were defined on the basis of the presence of a child who was not recorded on the census form as the son or daughter of one of the parents, whereas a child was defined as a stepchild if she or he was recorded as such on the census form.[18]

Qualifications

In a similar way to Table 3.6, Table 3.7 splits the results for stepfamilies from Table 3.5 according to whether a child is or is not a stepchild. The general difference between male children and female children is once again apparent. However, unlike the findings for the percentage in full-time education, the differences between stepchildren and non-stepchildren are consistent for male children and female children, depending on the type of stepfamily.

For children of each sex living in married couple stepfamilies, a larger percentage of stepchildren have qualifications at Level 2 or higher compared with non-stepchildren. Again, these non-stepchildren are only those with currently resident stepsiblings. For children of each sex living in cohabiting couple stepfamilies the opposite is observed, with a smaller percentage of stepchildren than of non-stepchildren having qualifications at Level 2 or higher. As noted earlier, this finding may be contingent upon the ways in which stepfamilies and stepchildren were identified in the 2001 Census.

Some studies focusing on children's family type when they were aged 16 have found the impact of parental divorce or parental absence to apply only to children living in stepfamilies and not to children living in lone parent families. One study that used NCDS data found an impact net of background characteristics, although this corresponded only to male children whose parents

Table 3.6

Student status of 17-year-olds[1] in stepfamilies according to family type, stepchild status and sex, 2001

Great Britain   Percentages

	Male			Female		
	In full-time education (per cent)	Not in full-time education (per cent)	Base	In full-time education (per cent)	Not in full-time education (per cent)	Base
Married couple stepfamily	53.6	46.4	25,198	65.8	34.2	22,989
Stepchild	53.1	46.9	20,455	66.3	33.7	18,671
Not a stepchild	55.4	44.6	4,743	64.1	35.9	4,318
Cohabiting couple stepfamily	49.5	50.5	14,515	63.4	36.6	13,040
Stepchild	46.3	53.7	5,273	61.2	38.8	4,888
Not a stepchild	51.4	48.6	9,242	64.7	35.3	8,152

1 Single individuals aged 17 who are not lone parents.

Source: 2001 Census, Office for National Statistics; General Register Office for Scotland

Table **3.7**

Percentage of 17-year-olds[1] in stepfamilies with qualifications at Level 2 or higher according to family type, stepchild status and sex, 2001

England and Wales | Percentages

	Male			Female		
	Qualifications at Level 2 or higher (per cent)	Qualifications- below Level 2 (per cent)	Base	Qualifications at Level 2 or higher (per cent)	Qualifications below Level 2 (per cent)	Base
Married couple stepfamily	53.2	46.8	23,425	65.6	34.4	21,404
Stepchild	53.8	46.2	19,038	66.6	33.4	17,417
Not a stepchild	50.2	49.8	4,387	61.2	38.8	3,987
Cohabiting couple stepfamily	50.6	49.4	13,417	64.3	35.7	12,088
Stepchild	46.7	53.3	4,905	61.5	38.5	4,545
Not a stepchild	52.8	47.2	8,512	65.9	34.1	7,543

1 Single individuals aged 17 who are not lone parents.

Source: 2001 Census, Office for National Statistics

had divorced and who were living in a stepfamily at age 16.[19] Focusing both on the occurrence of parental divorce or death between ages 7 and 16, and on family structure at age 16, this study found a significant reduction in the likelihood of staying on at school at age 16 for such children. Research using the BCS found that, once family income had been controlled for, there was a lower likelihood of obtaining any qualifications, and also a lower likelihood of obtaining five 'O' levels (or an equivalent of this), among children living in stepfamilies at age 16 as compared with children living in intact families.[20] The same study found that there was no such difference corresponding to children living in lone parent families at age 16.

Gender differences in education

With regard to gender, the pattern in Table 3.5 is similar to that in Table 3.3b. The percentage of female children with qualifications at Level 2 or above is considerably higher than that for male children for each family type. The variations by family type are similar for each sex. It is not surprising that a larger percentage of female children in full-time education is echoed by a larger percentage of female children with Level 2 or higher qualifications. The difference between female children and male children is of a similar order of magnitude for the qualification percentages as for the percentages in full-time education. Figure 3.8 shows in more detail how the gender differences vary between different family types. It compares gender differences in the percentage in full-time education (Table 3.3b) with gender differences in the percentage with qualifications at Level 2 or higher (Table 3.5).

Figure **3.8**

Differences between female and male children in percentage points, 2001

Percentage points

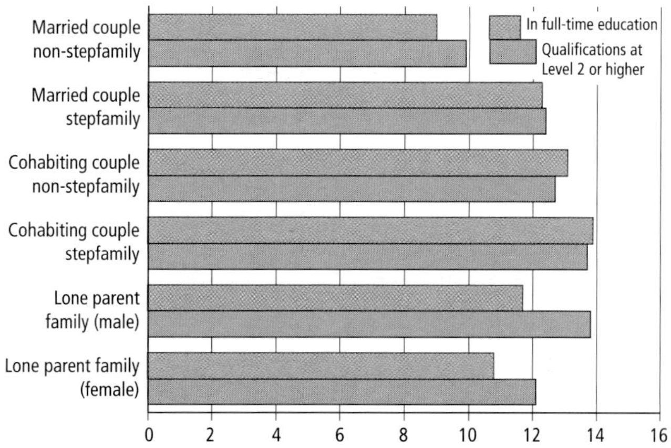

Note: This figure shows the differences between the percentages for female and male children aged 17 (male subtracted from female). The percentages are shown in Table 3.3b and Table 3.5.

The general differences between male children and female children have already been identified. Figure 3.8 is of interest because it shows how these differences vary by family type. The most striking finding is that there are smaller differences between male children and female children in married couple non-stepfamilies. In other words, the shortfalls for male children compared to female children are not as large (less than 10 percentage points). Conversely, in cohabiting couple families, the differences between male children and female children are larger. For cohabiting couple stepfamilies, the difference is close to 14 percentage points for both qualifications at Level 2 or higher and full-time education.

Box 2

The NSSEC is a classification system introduced by the Office for National Statistics in 2001, with eight classes used for most analyses. Findings presented in this chapter, however, apply only to those cases in which an occupation for the Household Reference Person could be coded and classified, and thus in this case correspond to seven NSSEC categories. The eighth category, people who have never worked and the long-term unemployed, has been excluded.[21]

NSSEC categories are defined as follows:

- classes 1 and 2 include managerial and professional occupations

- classes 3, 4 and 5 comprise intermediate occupations, small employers, own account workers, and lower supervisory and technical occupations

- classes 6 and 7 include semi-routine and routine occupations[22]

Socio-economic differences

Children in education

The differences in educational outcomes between family types may reflect differences between the distributions of socio-economic or educational characteristics of adults within each of the family types. Such characteristics are known to have an impact on children's educational outcomes.[23] Ideally, the educational outcomes of children within families would be compared to the educational levels of their parents. Owing to issues of data and comparability, it was not possible to carry

out an appropriate analysis of this sort. Instead, this chapter examines the relationship between children's educational outcomes and their household NSSEC (National Statistics Socio-Economic Classification) categories. These are defined in Box 2.

The NSSEC category for a household is based on the occupation of the Household Reference Person (HRP). Thus, in the case of households where the HRP does not belong to a child's family unit, this measure does not relate to one of the child's parents, although this situation appears to be quite unusual.[24] In addition, even if the HRP belongs to a child's family unit, he or she may be the child's step-parent rather than his or her biological parent. Furthermore, consideration should be given to the appropriateness of the NSSEC measure itself. For example, it may not be the most suitable measure of a family's socio-economic circumstances.

Figure 3.9a shows the percentage of 17-year-old male children in full-time education according to three bands of NSSEC categories while Figure 3.9b is the equivalent chart for female children aged 17. Based on the same data as Table 3.3b, these charts represent a more detailed version of Figure 3.3a.[25] NSSEC Classes 1 and 2, which include managerial and professional occupations, are banded together. The other two bands are NSSEC Classes 6 and 7, which include semi-routine and routine occupations, and the remaining three classes, containing intermediate occupations, NSSEC Classes 3, 4 and 5.[22]

Figures 3.9a and 3.9b show pronounced differences between NSSEC bands in the percentage of children in full-time education. Broadly consistent for male children and female children, these

Figure **3.9a** and **3.9b**

Percentage of children aged 17 in full-time education according to family type and household NSSEC, 2001

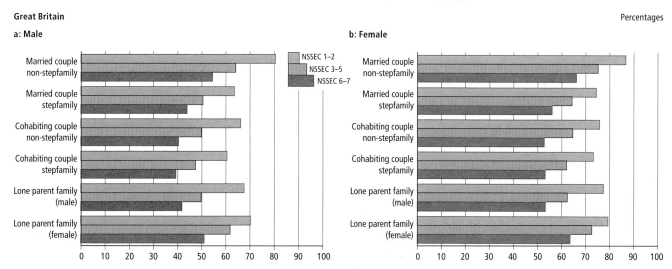

Great Britain   Percentages

Source: 2001 Census, Office for National Statistics; General Register Office for Scotland

differences correspond to larger percentages in full-time education in the higher bands of NSSEC classes. There are more children in full-time education in families with a Household Reference Person in NSSEC 1 or 2 as opposed to NSSEC 3, 4 or 5. The difference is approximately 10 to 15 percentage points. Between families in NSSEC 3, 4 or 5 and in NSSEC 6 or 7, the difference is of a slightly smaller magnitude, at just below 10 percentage points.

The differences between family types visible in Figures 3.9a and 3.9b are for the most part similar to those visible in Figure 3.3a. Generally, the lowest percentage of children in full-time education corresponds to male children in cohabiting couple families, and the highest percentage of children in full-time education corresponds to married couple non-stepfamilies. However, for the lower NSSEC bands, there is a markedly smaller difference between married couple non-stepfamilies and female lone parent families than is visible in Figure 3.3a.

For the second and third NSSEC bands the difference is less than a third of that visible in Figure 3.3a. Comparing female lone parent families with married couple non-stepfamilies, much of the shortfall visible in Figure 3.3a in the percentage of 17-year-olds who are in full-time education can be attributed to household NSSEC. Nevertheless, for children in female lone parent families belonging to NSSEC 1 or 2, there remains a marked shortfall. This finding is consistent for each of England, Scotland and Wales.[7]

More generally, a comparison between the results presented in Figures 3.9a and 3.9b and in Figure 3.3a indicates that the differences between married couple non-stepfamilies and the other types of family tend to diminish in magnitude once the NSSEC band of the Household Reference Person has been taken into account. However, the reduction is in most cases relatively small (about a tenth), although the differences between the percentages for married couple non-stepfamilies and for cohabiting couple non-stepfamilies diminish, on average, by over a fifth. A few differences increase in magnitude.

For the percentage in full-time education, the gap between NSSEC 1 or 2 and NSSEC 3, 4 or 5 is substantially greater for male children than for female children for all family types except female lone parent families. The impact of this aspect of a family's socio-economic characteristics thus appears to be greater for male children than for female children.

It is worth noting that occupational segregation by sex, together with intra-generational occupational mobility and movement between family types over the life course, have a potential impact on the findings. These factors mean that female lone parent families may have a substantially different distribution of

Table **3.10**

Differences between the percentages of female and male children aged 17 in full-time education according to family type and household NSSEC band, 2001

Great Britain   Percentage points

	Percentage point difference between female and male children		
	NSSEC 1–2	NSSEC 3–5	NSSEC 6–7
Married couple non-stepfamily	6.1	11.1	11.7
Married couple stepfamily	10.9	13.9	12.1
Cohabiting couple non-stepfamily	9.7	14.7	12.4
Cohabiting couple stepfamily	12.7	14.6	13.9
Lone parent family (male)	9.9	12.7	11.4
Lone parent family (female)	9.2	10.9	12.6

Source: 2001 Census, Office for National Statistics; General Register Office for Scotland

NSSEC classes to any families that the lone parents belonged to in the past. In consequence, there is a sense in which comparisons between female lone parent families and the other family types may not constitute a comparison of like with like.

Gender differences in education

Table 3.10 shows the differences between the percentages of male children and female children aged 17 in full-time education according to family type. The differences are positive, indicating that the percentages for female children are higher than those for male children for all family types. Married couple non-stepfamilies in NSSEC 1 or 2 show the smallest difference, which is 6.1 percentage points. The largest differences are for both types of cohabiting couple family in NSSEC 3, 4 or 5, and are 14.6 and 14.7 percentage points.

Overall, the variation in gender differences between family types is more pronounced for the higher bands of socio-economic classes, in particular for NSSEC 1 or 2. There are larger gender differences corresponding to NSSEC 3, 4 or 5 than for NSSEC 6 or 7. This is the case for all family types except married couple non-stepfamilies and female lone parent families. Thus the relationship between NSSEC, gender and the percentage of children in full-time education is relatively complex.

Qualifications

A similar analysis comparing NSSEC bands can be carried out focusing on qualifications at Level 2 or higher. Figures 3.11a and 3.11b show pronounced differences between NSSEC bands in the percentage of children with qualifications at Level 2 or higher. These differences are broadly consistent for male and female children, and reflect larger percentages of children with

Figure **3.11a** and **3.11b**

Percentage of children aged 17 with qualifications at Level 2 or higher according to family type and household NSSEC, 2001

England and Wales   Percentages

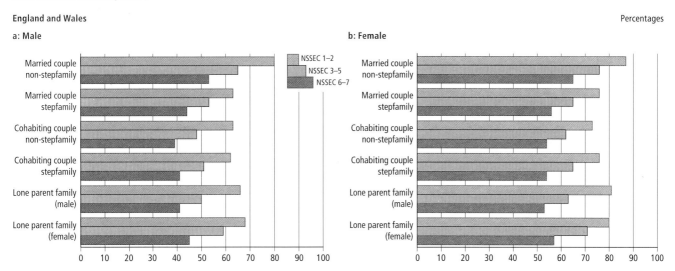

Source: 2001 Census, Office for National Statistics

such qualifications in the higher NSSEC bands. For all combinations of a child's sex and family type, there are more children with Level 2 or higher qualifications in families with a Household Reference Person in NSSEC 1 or 2 as opposed to NSSEC 3, 4 or 5. In most cases the difference is between 10 to 15 percentage points. The difference between families belonging to NSSEC 3, 4 or 5 and to NSSEC 6 or 7 is of a similar magnitude, though on average slightly smaller.

When considering qualifications, the differences between family types are similar to those seen above for full-time education. The lowest percentages of children with qualifications at Level 2 or higher correspond to male children in one or other form of cohabiting couple family. The highest percentages of children with qualifications at Level 2 or higher correspond to married couple non-stepfamilies. A difference between the results shown in Figures 3.11a and 3.11b and the earlier results relating to the proportion in full-time education is that female lone parent families have markedly lower percentages of children with qualifications at Level 2 or higher than married couple non-stepfamilies for all NSSEC bands.

However, female lone parent families still rank second among the family types for both sexes and in all NSSEC bands, with the exception of female children in households in NSSEC 1 or 2. For this latter group, male lone parent families have the second highest percentage (81 per cent). For the proportion in full-time education, a larger gap between NSSEC 1 or 2 and NSSEC 3, 4 or 5 was evident for male children than for female children. This pattern is also evident for qualifications. The gap is particularly substantial for both married couple and cohabiting couple non-stepfamilies, and for male lone parent families.

The differences visible in Figures 3.11a and 3.11b between married couple non-stepfamilies and the other types of family are in many instances smaller than the corresponding differences presented in Table 3.5. Differences between family types in the percentages of 17-year-olds possessing qualifications at Level 2 or higher thus tend to diminish in magnitude once the NSSEC band of the Household Reference Person has been taken into account. This echoes the findings discussed earlier relating to the proportion in full-time education. Once again, the most notable change is in the differences between the percentages for married couple non-stepfamilies and for female lone parent families. For each of the six combinations of NSSEC band and

Table **3.12**

Differences between the percentages of female and male children aged 17 with qualifications at Level 2 or higher according to family type and household NSSEC band, 2001

England and Wales   Percentage points

	Percentage point difference between female and male children		
	NSSEC 1–2	NSSEC 3–5	NSSEC 6–7
Married couple non-stepfamily	7.1	11.4	12.0
Married couple stepfamily	12.8	12.0	12.0
Cohabiting couple non-stepfamily	9.8	13.4	15.4
Cohabiting couple stepfamily	13.7	14.1	13.1
Lone parent family (male)	15.2	12.8	12.3
Lone parent family (female)	11.7	12.0	12.0

Source: 2001 Census, Office for National Statistics

sex, the difference between these two types of family is reduced from that presented in Table 3.5 by a proportion of between a third and two-thirds. The reduction in the differences is of a similar magnitude for England and for Wales.[7]

The differences between the percentages for married couple non-stepfamilies and for cohabiting couple non-stepfamilies diminish on average by about a quarter when NSSEC band is taken into account, and the differences between married couple non-stepfamilies and the remaining three family types diminish on average by at least a tenth. Overall, slightly more of the difference between married couple non-stepfamilies and the other family types is accounted for by NSSEC band when the focus is on qualifications rather than on full-time education.

Gender differences in qualifications

Table 3.12 shows the differences between the percentages of male children and female children aged 17 with qualifications at Level 2 or higher. The positive values show that the percentages for female children are higher than for male children for all family types and NSSEC bands. As with the proportion in full-time education (Table 3.10), the smallest difference is for married couple non-stepfamilies in NSSEC 1 or 2, and is 7.1 percentage points. For qualifications, the largest differences are for cohabiting couple non-stepfamilies in NSSEC 6 or 7 (15.4 percentage points) and male lone parent families in NSSEC 1 or 2 (15.2 percentage points). The corresponding differences in the proportion in full-time education were 12.4 and 9.9 percentage points respectively.

The variations in the difference across NSSEC bands can be classified into three patterns. The first pattern, for male lone parent families, is a greater difference between male and female children in the higher NSSEC bands (where NSSEC 1 or 2 is the highest band). The second pattern is where there is a greater difference between male and female children in the lower NSSEC bands. This is the case for non-stepfamilies, both married couple and cohabiting couple. All other family types exhibit the third pattern, a reasonably consistent difference between male and female children for each NSSEC band.

Overall differences between the proportions with qualifications and in full-time education

A comprehensive assessment of the relationship between having qualifications and being in full-time education would require other data sources and a more detailed analysis. For example, it would not be sufficient to use the possession of qualifications at Level 2 or higher as the only indicator of qualifications. Additionally, a fuller analysis would need to examine whether the exclusion from this analysis of part-time education and education in the workplace influences its findings. All of this is beyond the scope of this chapter.

Notwithstanding the limitations of the data analysed in this chapter, it is still interesting to compare the proportion in full-time education with the proportion with Level 2 or higher qualifications. The results presented in Figures 3.13a and 3.13b have been produced by subtracting the percentage with qualifications at Level 2 or higher from the percentage in

Figure **3.13a** and **3.13b**

A comparison for 17-year-olds between the percentage in full-time education and the percentage with qualifications at Level 2 or higher, 2001

England and Wales   Percentage points

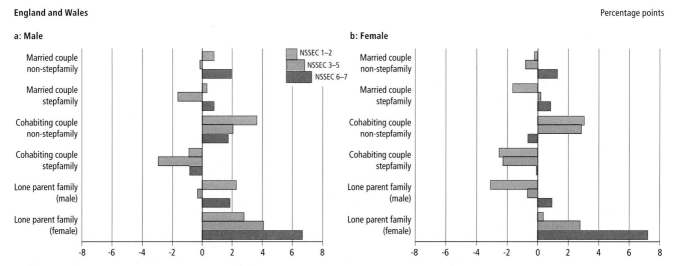

Note: The results in these figures have been obtained by subtracting the percentage with qualifications at Level 2 or higher from the percentage in full-time education. Therefore, positive numbers show a higher percentage in full-time education.

Source: 2001 Census, Office for National Statistics

full-time education. Therefore, positive numbers show a higher percentage in full-time education.[26,27]

Focusing on the largest differences and on consistent sets of differences within family types, the key features of Figures 3.13a and 3.13b can be summarised as follows:

A larger percentage of children in full-time education:

- All subgroups of children in cohabiting couple non-stepfamilies except female children in NSSEC 6 or 7

- Children in female lone parent families (although the difference is small for female children in NSSEC 1 or 2)

A larger percentage of children with Level 2 or higher qualifications:

- All subgroups of children in cohabiting couple stepfamilies (although the difference is small for female children in NSSEC 6 or 7)

- Female children in NSSEC 1 or 2 in male lone parent families

The above findings suggest that for children aged 17 in full-time education, the level of qualifications already obtained depends upon family type and household NSSEC. More specifically, there appear to be particular disparities between having qualifications at Level 2 or higher and being in full-time education for children in both types of cohabiting couple family and in female lone parent families (especially where the latter are in NSSEC 6 or 7). A similar finding by a study using data from the Youth Cohort Studies (YCS) indicated that children from female lone parent families are more likely to stay on in education at age 16 than are children from other types of families, once educational attainment has been controlled for.[28] Further research would be needed to understand these patterns.

PART TWO: Education and marital formation

Earlier studies have shown education to be associated with age at first marriage. Research in the 1980s using the National Survey of Health and Development (NSHD), a longitudinal study of the 1946 birth cohort, showed that the average age at first marriage rose as highest qualification level increased. It was found to be particularly high for people with degrees. Graduates, especially graduate women, were disproportionately likely to be single at age 36, whereas women with no qualifications were very unlikely to still be single, although this was not the case for men with no qualifications.[29, 30]

More recently, research using the NCDS has provided a detailed account of the relationship between education and partnership formation among the 1958 birth cohort. For both sexes, and controlling for various other factors, the likelihood of entry into marriage or cohabitation by age 23 diminished with increasing age at leaving school.[31] People with no qualifications and those

with degree level qualifications both showed different behaviour from those with intermediate levels of qualifications. For example the study also found, with regard to partnership formation between ages 23 and 32, a lower likelihood of direct transitions to marriage among people (of either sex) with no qualifications. These people might be remaining single or cohabiting. Men and women with degree level qualifications were found to delay partnership formation by remaining single until their mid-to-late twenties, when they tended to cohabit rather than marrying directly. The authors suggested that a move away from the parental home, which often accompanies higher education, may encourage entry into cohabitation.

Existing research has also documented marked changes in patterns of marital formation over the three decades preceding the 2001 Census. Examinations of trends in marital formation must be alert to the distinction between marriage timing and the proportion ever marrying. Trends in the former can easily be misinterpreted as trends in the latter, and vice versa. A recent study of twentieth century marriage trends in England and Wales has suggested that some of the decline in marriage rates since 1970, and hence in period-based measures of the proportion ever marrying, has been induced by increases in age at first marriage in cohorts born from the 1940s onwards. Nevertheless, the study estimates that the proportion of the 1971 birth cohort ever marrying will be only 77 per cent for women and 73 per cent for men, as compared with figures of 92 per cent and 89 per cent for the cohort born twenty years earlier.[32] Cohabitation prevalence has been shown to have increased substantially in Great Britain since 1970, including cohabitation as a precursor or alternative to first marriage.[33]

Existing research provides limited information relating to changes over time in the impact of education on marital formation. Research using the NCDS and the BCS has found evidence of continuities in class differences in partnership formation, these in part being a reflection of the ongoing impact of educational inequalities.[34] However, another analysis of BHPS data found evidence of changes in the relationship between parental occupations and partnership formation.[35] Such changes might reflect changes in the relationship between education and partnership formation.

Highest level of qualifications and marriage or cohabitation by given ages

Census tabulations can be used to examine the relationship between education and marital formation via an analysis of the proportions of individuals of a given age who have ever married, according to their highest level of qualifications. These proportions reflect both the distributions of age at first marriage within different birth cohorts and the proportion of each cohort who will eventually marry. Thus, interpretations of such

Box 3

Identifying highest level of qualifications from the census

The highest level of qualifications variable uses both the educational and vocational qualifications question and the professional qualifications question.

- No qualifications: no academic or professional qualifications.

- Level 1: one or more 'O' levels/CSEs/GCSEs (any grade); NVQ level 1; Foundation GNVQ; or equivalents.

- Level 2: five or more 'O' levels; 5+ CSEs (grade 1); five or more GCSEs (grade A – C); 1+ 'A' levels/'AS' levels; NVQ level 2; Intermediate GNVQ; or equivalents.

- Level 3: two or more 'A' levels; four or more 'AS' levels; Higher School Certificate; NVQ level 3; Advanced GNVQ; or equivalents.

- Level 4/5: First degree; Higher Degree; NVQ levels 4-5; HNC; HND; Qualified Teacher Status; Qualified Medical Doctor; Qualified Dentist; Qualified Nurse, Midwife, Health Visitor; or equivalents.

- Other qualifications/level unknown: other qualifications (for example City and Guilds); other professional qualification.[10]

Table **3.14**

Highest level of qualifications by sex for individuals aged 25, 35 and 45, 2001

United Kingdom — Percentages

	Age 25	Age 35	Age 45
Men			
None	11.6	16.4	26.3
Other[1]	3.1	4.1	10.7
Level 1/2	37.7	46.4	31.6
Level 3	13.5	7.9	7.5
Level 4/5	34.1	25.2	23.8
Base	346,603	459,115	378,319
Women			
None	10.0	15.1	29.9
Other[1]	2.1	2.2	5.1
Level 1/2	37.5	50.0	34.0
Level 3	13.6	8.5	7.2
Level 4/5	36.8	24.3	23.8
Base	357,382	475,101	384,535

1. The 'Other' level of qualifications is specific to England and Wales.

Source: 2001 Census, Office for National Statistics; General Register Office for Scotland; Northern Ireland Statistics and Research Agency

proportions need to acknowledge that those who have not yet married may marry later, but alternatively may not marry at all.

The analysis of marital formation in contemporary society is further complicated by the growth of cohabitation as a precursor or alternative to legal marriage, and the fact that data sources such as the census do not permit individuals who have previously cohabited to be distinguished from other single people living alone. When analysing the relationship between education

Box 4

Identifying partnership (marital and cohabiting) status

In order to identify the partnership status of individuals and to examine the relationship between this and highest level of qualifications, two census tables were used, one showing legal marital status and one focusing on living arrangements. The aim was to allocate individuals to three different partnership status categories:

1. ever married

2. single (never married) and cohabiting

3. single (never married) and not cohabiting

The first table, focusing on legal marital status, was used to identify those who had ever married (1) by a given age. This was achieved by aggregating the married, re-married, separated, widowed and divorced categories. The remaining individuals were single and had never married. A second table, based on living arrangements, was used, in combination with the first table, to divide these single people into those who were cohabiting (2) and those who were not (3).

This subdivision of single people is an approximation. There is an inconsistency between the two tables used, in that the legal marital status table includes individuals who were not living in households (such as those in communal establishments) but the living arrangements table does not. It was therefore assumed that all individuals not living in households were single (and had never married), which allowed the number of single people (living in households) who were cohabiting to be estimated. This was achieved by adding together the number of single people in households who were not cohabiting and the (estimated) number of single people not living in households, and subtracting the result from the total number of single people. Since the number of single people not living in households was over-estimated, the estimated number of single people who were cohabiting is consequently an under-estimate. However, the degree of under-estimation can be shown to be relatively small.[36]

and marital formation, an additional complication is that highest level of qualifications is not a characteristic that is fixed over time. Changes are fairly frequent within the first few years of adult life, and may feasibly occur at any point in time thereafter.

Key features of the relationship between highest level of qualifications and marital formation can be illustrated by focusing on three specific ages separated by ten year intervals. The use of census data allows this to be done without the sampling error that can adversely affect the reliability of sample survey data corresponding to small subgroups within the population. Census results can be viewed as representative of people of these specific ages within the UK population.

Box 3 describes how the highest level of qualifications measure is constructed from census information. Table 3.14 shows the highest levels of qualifications achieved by individuals of each sex within three census age cohorts: those aged 25, those aged 35 and those aged 45.[37] By age 25, changes in individuals' highest levels of qualification have become relatively infrequent. The table shows that members of the younger cohorts tend to have higher qualifications, particularly individuals aged 25.

Ever married

The method used to calculate numbers of individuals according to partnership (marital and cohabiting) status is outlined in Box 4. For each of the three age cohorts, Figure 3.15a and Figure 3.15b show the percentage ever married according to highest level of qualifications.[38] These charts illustrate both patterns of marital formation and the ways in which these vary according to gender. First, older people are more likely to have ever married.

There is a larger difference between the percentages of individuals who have ever married when ages 25 and 35 are compared than there is when ages 35 and 45 are compared. This holds true for both men and women. Second, women are more likely to have ever married than men, particularly women aged 25, who are almost twice as likely to have ever married as men, at any level of qualifications.

Looking at the relationship between the percentage ever married and highest level of qualifications, there are distinct differences between the three cohorts. For those aged 25, the percentage of individuals with Level 4 or 5 qualifications who have ever married is markedly lower than for other qualification levels. For both men and women, it is approximately half of the percentage for individuals with no qualifications. In general, for those aged 25, the percentage ever married is lower for each level of qualifications than for the preceding level.

The patterns of percentages for 35-year-olds are rather different. For both sexes, the highest percentage ever married corresponds to Level 1 or 2 qualifications, while those with no qualifications have the lowest percentages ever married. The percentages ever married for individuals with Level 4 or Level 5 qualifications fall in between these extremes. The differences between the percentage corresponding to Level 4 or 5 and the percentages corresponding to Levels 1 or 2 and Level 3 are greater for women than for men. Conversely, the difference between the percentages for no qualifications and Level 1 or 2 is somewhat greater for men than for women. Thus, the lower likelihood of marriage by age 35 for those with no qualifications appears more marked for men than for women, whereas the

Figure **3.15a** and **3.15b**

Percentages of men and women ever married according to highest level of qualifications for three age cohorts, 2001

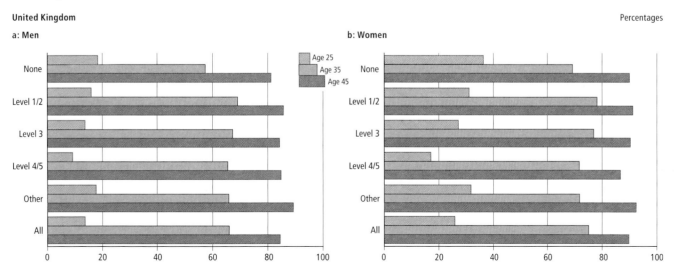

Note: These proportions include individuals who have ever married and are cohabiting.

Source: 2001 Census, Office for National Statistics; General Register Office for Scotland; Northern Ireland Statistics and Research Agency

lower likelihood of marriage by age 35 for those with Level 4 or 5 qualifications appears more marked for women than for men.

By age 45 the percentages ever married are relatively high. For women aged 45, the percentage ever married is 15 per cent higher than for those aged 35. For men, the percentage is 18 per cent higher. The most notable difference between men and women aged 45 is in the level of qualifications that has the lowest percentage ever married. For men, the lowest percentage is for individuals with no qualifications, 81 per cent, as compared to 86 per cent for those with Level 1 or 2 qualifications. For women the lowest is for individuals with Level 4 or 5 qualifications, 87 per cent, as compared to 91 per cent for those with Level 1 or 2 qualifications.

Single (never married) and cohabiting

Using the methodology outlined in Box 4, this section examines cohabitation by never-married individuals. Figure 3.16a and Figure 3.16b thus complement Figure 3.15a and Figure 3.15b by showing the percentages of men and women who have never married but are currently cohabiting according to their highest level of qualifications. It should be noted that, unless explicitly stated to the contrary, cohabitation as examined here excludes ever married individuals who are cohabiting (for example, divorced people who are cohabiting).

For individuals aged 25, the lowest percentage for each sex corresponds to individuals with no qualifications. Such individuals thus have the highest percentage ever married, but the lowest percentage currently cohabiting. The similarity between the cohabitation percentages for men and women decreases as highest level of qualifications increases. Women

with Level 4 or 5 qualifications are 6 per cent more likely to be cohabiting than men with the same level of qualifications. The percentage of these women who are cohabiting is similar to the percentages for women with Level 1 or 2 and Level 3 qualifications. However, given that the percentage of women with Level 4 or 5 qualifications who have never married is high, the percentage of Level 4 or 5 women who are currently cohabiting represents a smaller proportion of the subgroup of Level 4 or 5 women who have never married than is the case for the equivalent percentages for Levels 1 or 2 and Level 3.

For 35-year-olds there is a slight difference between men and women, with the cohabiting percentage for men being on average 3 per cent higher. However, the most noticeable feature of Figure 3.16a and Figure 3.16b for the 35-year-old cohort is the lack of variation between the different qualification levels, especially when compared with the 25-year-old cohort. However, if the percentages cohabiting are re-expressed as percentages of the individuals who have never married, then the highest rates of cohabitation are for individuals with qualifications at Level 1 or 2. Compared with Level 1 or 2, the rates for Level 3 and for Level 4 or 5 are somewhat lower (and are fairly similar to each other), and the rate for individuals with no qualifications is markedly lower.

For the 45-year-old cohort, the percentage of individuals cohabiting is very small, 2 per cent for women and 3 per cent for men. As such, there is little scope for variation between qualification levels in absolute terms. Nevertheless, the percentage cohabiting rises slightly with increasing qualifications (if the other qualifications category is disregarded). Looking at each cohabiting percentage as a proportion of those who have

Figure **3.16a** and **3.16b**

Percentages of men and women who are currently cohabiting but never married according to highest level of qualifications for three age cohorts, 2001

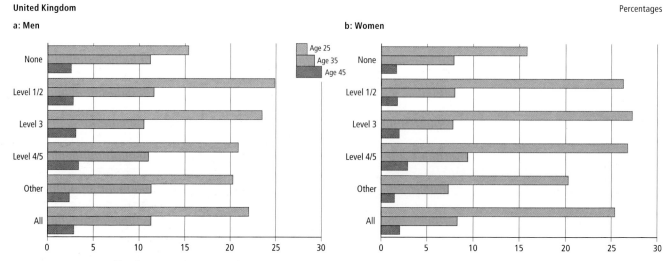

Source: 2001 Census, Office for National Statistics; General Register Office for Scotland; Northern Ireland Statistics and Research Agency

never married, the proportion currently cohabiting varies relatively little according to qualification level. The only distinctive result corresponds to men with no qualifications, for whom this proportion is lower.[39]

Comparing the three ages, younger individuals are much more likely to have never married but to be currently cohabiting. Furthermore, the cohabiting rate for 45-year-olds is still markedly lower than for the younger ages when viewed as a proportion of the never-married individuals of the relevant age. At all ages and for both sexes, the percentage who have never married but are cohabiting for individuals with no qualifications is relatively low. However, the relatively high percentage who have never married but are cohabiting for women with Level 4 or 5 qualifications at each age is partly a consequence of the low proportion of women with Level 4 or 5 qualifications who have married by each age. At ages 25 and 35, the percentage who have never married but are cohabiting for men with Level 1 or 2 qualifications is higher than for men with Level 4 or 5 qualifications. There is evidently not a straightforward tendency for the likelihood of cohabitation to increase as level of qualifications increases.

Single (never married) and not cohabiting

This section uses the same methodology as the two preceding sections (see Box 4) to look at the variation according to qualifications in the proportion of individuals who have never married and are not cohabiting. Figures 3.17a and 3.17b show that, for 25-year-olds of each sex, the pattern of percentages is U-shaped, with the lowest percentages of individuals who have never married and are not cohabiting corresponding to

Level 1 or 2 qualifications. Among the 35-year-olds, men and women with no qualifications are most likely to have never married and not be cohabiting. However, among the 45-year-olds, women with Level 4 or 5 qualifications and men with none are most likely to have never married and not be cohabiting.

On the basis of the results discussed in the two preceding sections and the results in this one, some cautious suggestions can be made regarding the relationship between education and marital formation. Men and women with no qualifications appear relatively likely to marry early (by age 25) but relatively unlikely to cohabit early. However, by age 35 men and women with no qualifications appear relatively unlikely to have married and this seems also to be true for men aged 45 with no qualifications. Overall, men and women with no qualifications seem to marry at a relatively diverse range of ages and, in the case of men, to be more likely not to marry by age 45. Men and women with Level 4 or 5 qualifications appear relatively unlikely to marry by age 25. By age 45, the gap in the likelihood of having married between the highest educational category and the lower categories disappears for men, but not for women. Thus men and women with Level 4 or 5 qualifications appear more likely to delay marriage. Women with Level 4 or 5 qualifications may also be less likely ever to marry, assuming that current marriage trends after age 45 do not change.

The above suggestions assume that the relationship between education and marital formation is consistent across the three age cohorts. It is worth noting that the patterns of age at first marriage for these three cohorts differ. Specifically, published marriage statistics for England and Wales[40] show that much greater proportions of men and women aged 35 and 45 at the

Figure **3.17a** and **3.17b**

Percentages of men and women who are never married and are not currently cohabiting according to highest level of qualifications for three age cohorts, 2001

United Kingdom

Percentages

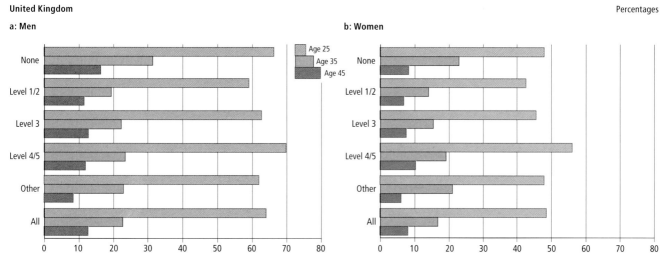

Source: 2001 Census, Office for National Statistics; General Register Office for Scotland; Northern Ireland Statistics and Research Agency

census date had married by age 25 than of men and women aged 25. They also show that a greater proportion of men and women aged 45 at the census date had married by age 35 than of men and women aged 35.

It cannot be established from the 2001 Census whether men and women who had never married and were not currently cohabiting had cohabited in the past. However, the General Household Survey[41] of 2001–2002 collected data on past cohabitation. These data suggest that, for the age range 30–49, 31 per cent of such men and 43 per cent of such women had cohabited in the past.[42] These findings suggest that the proportions of men and women aged 45 at the census date who had never married or cohabited with a partner are markedly lower than the proportions of such men and women who had never married and were not currently cohabiting (as shown in Figures 3.17a and 3.17b). For this reason, where possible, research on contemporary marriage should take account of both current and past cohabitation.

Conclusions

Educational outcomes and family type

The results presented in this chapter regarding the relationship between family type and educational outcomes are to a large extent consistent with previous research. Children living in married couple non-stepfamilies at age 17 were most likely to be in full-time education and to have Level 2 qualifications. Taking account of the NSSEC category of their households, however, showed that at least some of the difference between such families and other family types reflects socio-economic differences. In particular, controlling for household NSSEC eliminated much of the difference between married couple non-stepfamilies and female lone parent families.

There are, however, several aspects of the data that need to be borne in mind when interpreting the findings relating to family types and education. For example, the findings may be influenced by variations between family types in the ages at which children leave home. Furthermore, the comparisons between stepchildren and other children within stepfamilies must be viewed with caution, given the differences between the definitions of stepchildren and stepfamilies within the census.

The results in this chapter do not indicate that children aged 17 living in lone parent families are in the least favourable educational situation relative to children belonging to other family types. If anything, it is children in cohabiting couple families who appear least likely to be in full-time education and least likely to have achieved qualifications at Level 2 or higher, especially once household NSSEC has been controlled for. The findings of earlier studies suggest that controlling for additional socio-economic factors, such as financial difficulties, would have

further reduced the difference between female lone parent families and married couple non-stepfamilies. If information on household income had been available from the census, controlling for this might have resulted in comparable educational outcomes for lone parent families and for married couple non-stepfamilies. However, while differences in educational outcomes between family types may reflect differences between the distributions of socio-economic characteristics for each family type, they may also reflect the characteristics of the families that preceded many lone parent families and stepfamilies.

Differences in educational outcomes are apparent between stepfamilies and married couple non-stepfamilies. For the most part these persist after controlling for household NSSEC. Many of the 17-year-olds who were in stepfamilies at the census date will have experienced parental separation or divorce at an earlier stage and many will have spent time in a lone parent family. Thus, like the findings of some of the earlier studies, the results presented in this chapter may indicate that the impact on educational outcomes of parental divorce or experience of a lone parent family is more substantial for children who go on to live in stepfamilies.

However, the results also suggest that stepfamilies should not be viewed as a homogeneous family type. For example, within married couple stepfamilies, a larger proportion of male and female 17-year-old stepchildren have qualifications at Level 2 or higher than of equivalent non-stepchildren. Conversely, in cohabiting couple stepfamilies, a smaller proportion of stepchildren than non-stepchildren have qualifications at Level 2 or higher.

The findings indicate a gender difference in educational outcomes, whereby more 17-year-old female children than male children have qualifications at Level 2 or higher and more are in full-time education. This difference varies in magnitude according to family type and household NSSEC, and is smallest for married couple non-stepfamilies in NSSEC 1 or 2. For 17-year-olds in full-time education, the findings suggest that the level of qualifications already obtained may depend upon a combination of family type and household NSSEC. Thus, the impact of family type upon educational outcomes is complex, and is contingent upon both gender and socio-economic characteristics.

Education and marital formation

The findings relating to education and marital formation presented in this chapter are broadly equivalent to the findings of earlier research. Higher levels of qualifications have been shown to be associated with later marriage, but the relationship between education and marital formation appears to be complex. Men and women with no qualifications are relatively likely to marry early (by age 25) but relatively unlikely to cohabit early.

However, men and women aged 35 with no qualifications are less likely to have ever married than those with qualifications. This difference does not reflect a higher likelihood of cohabitation. At age 45, the individuals who are least likely to have ever married are men with no qualifications and women with qualifications at Level 4 or 5. Once again, there is no evidence that such individuals are disproportionately likely to have cohabited instead of marrying.

The results for women aged 45 are consistent with earlier studies that have shown female graduates, but not male graduates, to be more likely than individuals with lower qualifications never to marry. Furthermore, the results for men and women aged 35 suggest that this gender-specific effect of high qualifications on the likelihood of ever marrying is not, in the short term at least, going to disappear. However, the results for men and women aged 35 may indicate that the effect of having no qualifications on the likelihood of ever marrying will eventually cease to be gender-specific.

Comparisons between age cohorts using a cross-sectional study such as the census should be made with caution. In relation to this, it is worth referring to Table 3.14, which shows the different proportions in each qualifications category for each age cohort. It may be that variations between the results for people of different ages are because of generational differences; Table 3.14 shows that having no qualifications is markedly less common among the 25 and 35-year-olds than among the 45-year-olds. Conversely, having Level 4 or 5 qualifications is markedly more common among the 25-year-olds than among the 35- and 45-year-olds. As such, having no qualifications has become more distinctive and having Level 4 or 5 qualifications has become less distinctive, and this may have implications for the marital formation patterns corresponding to these categories.

Notes and references

1   The high value of the percentage in the not applicable category for lone parents with non-dependent children relates to families where the Family Reference Person is aged 75 or over.

2   Sigle-Rushton W, Hobcraft J and Kiernan K (2005), 'Parental divorce and subsequent disadvantage: A cross-cohort comparison', *Demography* 42.3, pp 427–446.

3   Blundell R, Dearden L, Goodman A and Reed H (1997), *Higher Education, Employment and Earnings in Britain*, Institute for Fiscal Studies: London.

4   An analysis of the relationship between family type and educational outcomes including these categories might be attempted using the 2001 Census Household Sample of Anonymised Records (SAR). However, allocating individuals in these categories to family types would be complex and could well prove impossible in many cases.

5   Comparable data were not available for Northern Ireland when this analysis was carried out.

6   These percentages are derived from 2001 Census data.

7   Analysis was carried out using 2001 Census data.

8   Research focusing on leaving home, and examining, among other things, the effects of qualifications and of family structure, has been carried out using European Community Household Panel (ECHP) data. See Iacovou M. (2001), *Leaving home in the European Union*, Working Papers of the Institute for Social and Economic Research, Paper 2001–18, University of Essex: Colchester.

9   However, the analysis in this part of the chapter is constrained by there being insufficient detail in the highest qualification variable as tabulated for Scotland and Northern Ireland to include these countries in the analysis.

10 Office for National Statistics (2004) *Census 2001 Definitions*, Palgrave Macmillan: Basingstoke.

11 For further information on imputation, see Office for National Statistics (2005), *Census 2001: Quality report for England and Wales*, Palgrave Macmillan: Basingstoke, available at: www.statistics.gov.uk/downloads/census2001/census_2001_quality_report.pdf

12 Gregg P and Machin S (1998), *Child development and success or failure in the youth labour market*, Centre for Economic Performance Discussion Paper No. 397, London School of Economics: London, available at: http://cep.lse.ac.uk/pubs/download/DP0397.pdf

13 Kiernan K (1997) *The Legacy of Parental Divorce: Social, economic and demographic experiences in adulthood*, Centre for Analysis of Social Exclusion (CASE) Paper No. 1, London School of Economics: London, available at: http://sticerd.lse.ac.uk/dps/case/cp/paper1.pdf

14 Gayle V, Berridge D and Davies R (2002), 'Young People's Entry into Higher Education: quantifying influential factors', *Oxford Review of Education*, 28.1, pp 5–20.

15 Ermisch J, Francesconi M and Pevalin D (2004), 'Parental partnership and joblessness in childhood and their influence on young people's outcomes', *Journal of the Royal Statistical Society (Series A)* 167.1, pp 69–101.

16 A sibling-difference approach to modelling the impact of family structure on educational outcomes allows the impact of other family characteristics, which are shared by all siblings but which are not explicitly included in the analysis, to be controlled for.

17 Ermisch J and Francesconi M (2001), 'Family Matters: Impacts of Family Background on Educational Attainment', *Economica* 68, pp 137–156.

18 Data from the 2001 Individual Sample of Anonymised Records (SAR) can be used to illustrate the resulting problem. They show that 29 per cent of individuals aged 16–18 in cohabiting couple stepfamilies were recorded on the census form as being unrelated to the Household Reference Person. This compared with less than 1 per cent of such individuals in married couple stepfamilies. However, these figures from the SAR are not fully consistent with the analysis in this chapter. This is because the Household Reference Person was not always a parent within the child's family unit. In addition, some individuals aged 16–18 within cohabiting couple stepfamilies were themselves parents. Nevertheless, it appears almost certain that some children living in cohabiting couple stepfamilies (as defined by the 2001 Census) who were not the child of one of the partners were not recorded on the census form as being a stepchild.

19 Ní Bhrolcháin M, Chappell R, Diamond I and Jameson C (2000), 'Parental divorce and outcomes for children: Evidence and interpretation', *European Sociological Review* 16.1, pp 67–91.

20 Ely M, West P, Sweeting H and Richards M (2000), 'Teenage family life, life chances, lifestyles and health: a comparison of two contemporary cohorts', *International Journal of Law, Policy and the Family*, 14.1, pp 1–30.

21 Data are not presented here for those cases where the Household Reference Person had never worked, was long-term unemployed, or was a full-time student, and for cases where an occupation was not coded and classified for the Household Reference Person, a total of just under 11 per cent of the cases in Table 3.3b.

22 Note that NSSEC Class 5 is sometimes aggregated with NSSEC 6 and 7 within a three class version of NSSEC, but for the purposes of this analysis it appears to share a greater similarity with NSSEC Classes 3 and 4.

23 Breen R and Jonsson J (2005) 'Inequality of opportunity in comparative perspective: recent research on educational attainment and social mobility', *Annual Review of Sociology* 31, pp 223–243.

24 An analysis of data from the 2001 Census Individual Sample of Anonymised Records (SAR) indicates that less than 4 per cent of children aged 16–18, who were not married or cohabiting, and who were living with a parent or parents, do not have a parent or step-parent as their Household Reference Person. While this indicates that an analysis using household NSSEC should be fairly robust, the number of children whose household NSSEC is not the same as that of their parent or parents may vary across different family types.

25 The percentages on which these figures are based are available from the author.

26 The percentages with qualifications at Level 2 or higher used in this calculation are those shown in Figures 3.11a and 3.11b. However, to achieve geographical comparability with these percentages, the percentages in full-time education used in this calculation are specific to England and Wales, rather than being those shown in Figures 3.9a and 3.9b, which relate to Great Britain.

27 These excesses and corresponding shortfalls do not, however, convey any information about any relationship that may exist between qualifications and being in full-time education.

28 Bradley S and Taylor J (2004), 'Ethnicity, educational attainment and the transition from school', *The Manchester School* 72.3, pp 317–346.

29 Kiernan K and Eldridge S (1987), 'Inter- and Intra-cohort variation in the timing of first marriage', *British Journal of Sociology* 38.1, pp 44–65.

30 Kiernan K (1988), 'Who Remains Celibate?', *Journal of Biosocial Science* 20.3, pp 253–264.

31 Berrington A and Diamond I (2000), 'Marriage or cohabitation: a competing risks analysis of first-partnership formation among the 1958 British birth cohort', *Journal of the Royal Statistical Society (Series A)* 163.2, pp 127–151.

32 Schoen R and Canudas-Romo V (2005), 'Timing effects on first marriage: Twentieth-century experience in England and Wales and the USA', *Population Studies* 59.2, pp 135–146.

33 Murphy M (2000), 'The evolution of cohabitation in Britain, 1960–95', *Population Studies* 54.1, pp 43–56.

34 Berrington A (2003), *Change and Continuity in Family Formation among Young Adults in Britain*, Social Statistics Research Centre Applications and Policy Working Paper A03/04, University of Southampton: Southampton, available at: http://eprints.soton.ac.uk/8139/01/ssrc-workingpaper-a03-04.pdf

35 Ermisch J and Francesconi M (1996), *Partnership Formation and Dissolution in Great Britain*, Working Papers of the ESRC Research Centre on Micro-social Change: Paper 96-10, University of Essex: Colchester.

36 The shortfalls for most combinations of age and highest level of qualifications can be assumed to be no more than 0.2 percentage points, rising to a maximum of 0.5 percentage points as age increases and highest level of qualifications decreases. In addition, further estimations were carried out, based upon the assumption that the distributions of marital status for individuals who were currently cohabiting and for individuals living outside households were the same within each sex and highest qualification combination. This assumption, which was likely to lead to an overestimation of the level of cohabitation among single people, led to percentages that were greater than those presented by a maximum of less than 1.0 percentage points. Moreover, a third set of estimations using distributional assumptions based on marital status data from the census theme table on communal establishment residents in England and Wales resulted in a maximum difference of 0.5 percentage points. (See Table T09 in: Office for National Statistics (2003), *Census 2001: National report for England and Wales part 1*, TSO: London, available at: www.statistics.gov.uk/downloads/census2001/National_report_ EW_Part1_Section3.pdf)

37 To allow findings to be presented corresponding to all the countries within the UK, no distinction is made in this section between highest qualifications at Levels 1 and 2.

38 The percentages on which these and subsequent figures are based can be supplied by the author.

39 This can only partially be explained by the differential shortfalls in the cohabiting percentages according to level of highest qualification mentioned earlier.

40 Table 3.36 in: Office for National Statistics (2005), *Marriage, Divorce and Adoption Statistics – 2002 (Series FM2 No. 30)*, Office for National Statistics: London, available at: www.statistics.gov.uk/downloads/theme_population/FM2no30/ FM2no30.pdf

41 Office for National Statistics, Social Survey Division, *General Household Survey, 2001–2002* (computer file), 3rd Edition, Colchester, Essex: UK Data Archive (distributor), October 2004, SN: 4646.

42 A more detailed tabulation is available from the author. Note that the General Household Survey collects data only from private households. Findings from this survey are subject to sampling error; this precluded a detailed analysis of the relationship between education and past cohabitation.

Family living arrangements and health

Mike Murphy

Chapter 4

Introduction

The family is one of the most important domains in people's lives. This chapter considers the relationship between family living arrangements and health. Particular attention is given to the most widely examined aspect, that between marital status and health (both mortality and morbidity). The nature of the relationship between family living arrangements and health is reviewed, and it is shown that, in general, married people have the best health, followed by the single, with the formerly-married having the worst. Analyses are presented on mortality by marital status, on variations in self-reported long-term illness from the 2001 Census, and across a number of different indicators of health status, self-reported and independently-measured, from the 2001 Health Survey for England.

Definitions

This chapter considers the relationship between family living arrangements and health. While 'family' is reasonably straightforward in statistical terms, referring to a co-resident group of close relatives,[1] 'health' is more complex to define and measure.[2] Health is defined by the World Health Organization[3] as a 'state of complete physical social and mental wellbeing and not merely the absence of disease or infirmity'. This definition of health has been further refined by the World Health Organization Quality of Life Group to include social integration, defining quality of life as:

> ...an individual's perception of their position in life in the context of the culture and value system in which they live and in relation to their goals, expectations, standards and concerns. It is a broad ranging concept affected in complex ways by the person's physical health, psychological state, level of independence, social relationships, and their relationships to salient features of their environment.[4]

Thus there are five concepts inherent in this definition:

- physical health
- mental health
- social functioning
- role functioning
- general wellbeing

However, in practice, health is normally defined in relation to self-assessed reports or externally measured indicators (including mortality). It is obvious that there **must** be a relationship between family living arrangements and health as defined above, since family is a major component of life satisfaction.[5]

The chapter will consider some of the previous findings of the relationship between health and family and explanations for these relationships. It will then present some new analysis of

the relationship between family and health using the 2001 Census and the 2001 Health Survey for England (HSE).

Health and family – previous findings

Previous analysis has focused on the relationship of one key family variable, marital status, and one key (ill-) health indicator, mortality. The relationship between these two variables has been the subject of detailed scientific investigation for a century and a half. In 1858, William Farr, the Superintendent of Statistics in the General Registrar's Office, found significantly lower mortality among the married than the unmarried in mid-19th century France, for women over age 30 and for men over age 20. Death rates for younger married women were not lower than for unmarried women, probably because of their higher risk of death in childbirth. 'Marriage is a healthy estate,' Farr concluded, 'if unmarried people suffer from disease in undue proportion, the have-been-married suffer still more. ... The single individual is more likely to be wrecked on his voyage than the lives joined together in matrimony'.[6]

Many studies of historical marriage and mortality data have shown the association between marriage and health is enduring and pervasive.[7] Married people have been found to have the best mental and physical health, followed by the single (never-married) and then the previously married.[8]

Generally, the health advantage of the married has been found to persist even when controlling for age, health behaviours, material resources acquired through marriage, and other relevant socio-demographic, health behaviour and health status factors.[9] Moreover, this advantage has been found in studies using a wide range of health indicators, including mortality, work disability, hospital admissions, length of hospital stay, and both acute and chronic limiting conditions.[10]

More recently, studies have shown that the mortality advantage of married people aged between 65 and 74,[11] and aged 75 and over, has increased relative to the non-married across a number of European countries, including Britain.[12] Marital status differentials were also found to be increasing in Finland.[13] There are many reasons for this relationship, and the strength of the association between marital status and health might be expected to vary according to age, sex, and cultural context.

Sex differences in relationships between marital status and health

Marriage appears to provide a greater protective effect for men than for women, and widowers experience greater excess mortality than widows.[14] However, women also gain some advantages. Married women aged 40–64 have significant health advantages over those who were unmarried, and mothers were healthier than those without children.[15]

Age differences in relationships between marital status and health

Some studies suggest that the relationship between health and marital status may be weaker in older age groups than for those in midlife.[16] Analysis of the US Longitudinal Study of Aging, a relatively large national sample of the private household population, found that never-married women had better health outcomes than their ever-married counterparts, a result the authors attributed to the fact that they have established a supportive social environment and had not experienced stressful life events such as widowhood or divorce.[17]

There are also a number of studies of elderly people that show, at least for the oldest age groups, that those living alone tend to be healthier than their counterparts living with adults other than a spouse. In some cases, they are even healthier than married adults.[18]

Household size and structure and other types of living arrangements

Evidence suggests that the benefits of marriage are emotional, financial and behavioural.[19] The social support of marriage affects health and well-being by mediating stress.[20] Marriage is not the only relationship or network that does this, and some benefits are more associated with household living arrangements than with marital status itself. The health status of cohabiting couples has been found to be more similar to married couples than to other groups.[21]

Poorer health among the formerly-married may be an outcome of the loss of social control, in that a spouse is no longer available to monitor the individual's health. Recently widowed or divorced men have been found to smoke more and experience greater weight loss than those who have never married, which may be a result of the strain of becoming unmarried rather than the state of being unmarried itself.[22] However, all unmarried men, not just the recently bereaved or divorced, had higher rates of alcohol intake than continuously married men, suggesting that increases in negative health behaviours among this group are not only a result of the stress of losing a spouse.

On the other hand, there is evidence that older people living alone may be selected for good, rather than poor, health. Data from the ONS Longitudinal Study (LS)[23] show that mortality rates in the period 1971–75 for men and women aged 30–49 (who were in one-person households in 1971), were respectively, 43 and 58 per cent higher than the average mortality rate for all men and women in that age group.[24] However, at ages 75 and over these ratios show below average mortality, with values of 3 per cent lower than the average for

men and 15 per cent for women. The ONS LS has also been used to show that the mortality of elderly women living alone was similar to that of women in married couple families and below that of lone parents or women not in a family but living with others.[25] The lower mortality experienced by the elderly who live alone, compared with that of individuals in other family and household types, implies that particularly healthy people are more likely to be selected into this living arrangement.

The changing pattern of mortality differentials by age of those living alone emphasises the difficulties in producing an overall summary index of the relationship between living arrangements and health. For example, very young adults living in a partnership, married or cohabiting, tend to be relatively disadvantaged in a number of ways, such as employment and education compared with those who are single.[26] To aggregate groups into particular classifications of living arrangements runs the risk of obscuring patterns by combining relatively advantaged and disadvantaged groups into a single category.

Divorce and family health

Among people whose marriages had broken down, past research has found that divorced and separated individuals had the highest rates of acute and limiting chronic conditions. They also had the most physician visits per year, the highest hospitalisation rates, and the longest hospital stays when compared to the other marital status groups.[27] A significantly increased hazard of dying among men who had recently divorced when compared to those who had made no recent marital status transitions has also been found, but this was not true for women.[28] There appears to be a sex differential in health within the divorced/separated marital status category.

Marital breakdown has a greater negative impact on the physical[29] and mental health[30] of women than on men. To a certain extent the relationship between divorce and poor health habits, such as smoking, may be traced to a common personality profile.[31] However, health habits alone cannot fully account for the health-enhancing effects of marriage. In a study that compared the health of separated or divorced men with that of married men, who were carefully matched in economic and occupational circumstances and had almost identical health behaviours, divorced and separated men had worse health and had poorer cellular immune system control than the married men.[9]

Children and family health

Most of the research on the physical health effects of divorce has focused on adults, not children, since children of divorced parents have been shown to suffer significantly worse health than the children of intact marriages. Parental divorce is not only associated with mental neurosis, but also helps foster 'various physical diseases, including cardiac disorders' later in their lives.[32]

Studies have found that children in intact two-parent families tend to have the best health.[33] A US study concluded that 'single mothers report poorer overall physical health for their children', and explained its findings by noting that many unmarried mothers live in poverty, which exposes their children to greater health risks. Additionally, a disproportionate number of single mothers are young and therefore more likely to bear an illness-prone premature infant.[34]

However, care is required before assuming that any effects are caused by family dissolution when comparing children in intact and disrupted families. The ideal comparison would be between children in two groups of families which were identical in every respect except that one group had experienced disruption and the other had not, but this is clearly unlikely to be the case. For example, families that dissolve because of parental divorce may be more likely to have a history of parental arguments, family stress and other similar effects. Furthermore, the results may show an association between child health effects and family dissolution, but this does not mean that family dissolution is the cause.

Like divorce, extra-marital childbearing appears linked to adverse health problems for children. In Britain, infant mortality rates in 2005 were 20 per cent higher for extra marital births registered by couples living at the same address (cohabiting couples), but 60 per cent higher for other births (registered by couples not at same address or with no father recorded on the birth certificate), compared with children born to married couples.[35] Rates of sudden infant death were twice as high for births outside as compared with births inside marriage, and rates of sudden infant death plus unascertained causes were three times as high.[36] While marriage exerts no 'direct causal influence on the outcome of pregnancy', a life course that includes marriage is likely to be healthier than one that does not. For example, unmarried mothers are more likely to smoke than married mothers.[37]

Mortality rates have been shown to be consistently lower for parents than for adults who are not parents, and for the married than for the unmarried, because marriage and parenthood both exert a 'deterrent effect on health-compromising behaviours' such as excessive drinking, drug use, risk-taking, and disorderly living. By providing a system of 'meaning, obligation, [and] constraint', family relationships markedly reduce the likelihood of unhealthy practices.[38]

Box 1

2001 Census questions on health and its interpretation

The 2001 Census asked:

Do you have any long-term illness, health problem or handicap which limits your daily activities or the work you can do? (include problems which are due to old age).

Although general questions of this kind are clearly limited, they have been found to correlate well at both the individual and the aggregate level with other indicators of health, such as doctor consultations and mortality.[39] Nevertheless they must be interpreted with caution, as explained in an international comparison of health surveys by the World Health Organization:

No gold standard measurement technique exists to assess all aspects of health or to assess what people perceive. Self-reported health is what individuals report within a survey to a lay interviewer. This may differ from what an individual perceives, particularly when specific incentives or sanctions influence reporting behaviour. Perceptions may differ from true health due to different definitions of health and wellbeing, different expectations for health and

different cognitive processes. Such differences reflect variations in cultural and gender norms, knowledge and information, and other factors that shape people's perceptions. ... More surprising is that users of household interview surveys often ignore these limitations and interpret self-reported data at face value. ... studies have documented that sub-populations with lower expectations for health (such as the elderly) or less exposure to what constitutes full health (such as those with lower socio-economic levels) actually report themselves in better health in comparison to tested or observed health status, or other external criteria.[40]

If group A reports twice as many people with a long-standing illness, it does not mean that they are twice as ill, nor does a doubling of such reported ill health by the same group over time mean that there is twice as much ill health in the latter period. For example, among those aged under 45, there was a substantial increase in the proportions reporting long-standing illness in the General Household Survey between the 1970s and 2000.[41] On the other hand, the census data set is much larger, has less non-response and includes the institutional population. The large size makes it possible to analyse specific small groups such as *de facto* marital status groups and lone parents.

Family and health in 2001

Data sources

The 2001 Census repeated a question first asked in the 1991 Census on limiting long-term illness, the first health-related question in a census since 1911. (In 2001 there was also a question on self-assessment of a person's general health over the 12 months before the census, but this chapter does not consider this question.) Thus information on health status comes from responses to the question on limiting long-term illness (see Box 1).

The Health Survey for England (HSE) was instituted in 1991. Since the administration of the health service is different Scotland, Wales and Northern Ireland, no source of comprehensive data for Great Britain exists. The 2001 Survey used here included 14,838 adults aged 20 and over in private households and all eligible members of the sample households were included. As well as self-reported morbidity, the survey also included questions on a variety of topics such as physical health measurements and blood analyses. While this does not provide detailed information about the joint dynamics of health and living arrangements, it does provide much more detailed data on patterns of morbidity than are available from alternative sources such as the General Household Survey.[42]

Researchers have recognised the problems of interpreting self-reported data.[40] An obvious example is that women tend to report more illness yet score better on objective indicators such as blood pressure, cholesterol level, alcohol and tobacco consumption and Body Mass Index. They also tend to experience lower mortality rates.[27]

The problems of interpreting self-reported data mean that there are considerable advantages in being able to compare different aspects of subjective and objective measures of health for the same sample. The HSE contains a much wider range of health indicators, both self-reported and objective. These are not only for a narrow definition of health, but also aspects such as perceptions of social support, and psychological health, which is a major component of global disease. For example, the Global Burden of Disease Study found that of the ten leading causes of disability worldwide in 1990, measured in years lived with a disability, five were psychiatric conditions: unipolar depression, alcohol use, bipolar affective disorder (manic depression) schizophrenia and obsessive-compulsive disorder.[43]

Data to establish the exact form of the patterns of **causality** between living arrangements and health cannot be established from the sorts of data discussed above. In addition, some of the associations may be influenced by socio-economic factors.

This report confines attention to the associations between aspects of these two domains and suggesting plausible hypothesis for the observed relationships.

Health and living arrangements: measures available

One problem in assessing the strength of the relationship between living arrangements and health is that both aspects are multidimensional. In the case of health, the various measures have already been mentioned. Box 2 explains which information has been used from the HSE.

For living arrangements, two main variables are used: partnership status (married or cohabiting; separated, widowed or divorced) and family circumstances (whether in private household or communal establishment; in couple or lone parent family; and the presence or absence of children).

Mortality by marital status

From 2002 to 2004, for every age group above age 30 the recorded mortality rates are lowest in the married category (apart from ages 85 and over for single males, although data by marital status at older ages is not as reliable). At ages under 30, the numbers of people widowed and divorced are relatively small so the values are not shown (Table 4.2).

Between ages 30 and 50, single men have death rates about three times that of married men, and single women have rates about double those of married women. At these young ages, widowed people have particularly high relative rates compared with married people (although because rates are low, the absolute difference in rates is less substantial). In part, this is likely to be associated with spouses' joint experience of events, such as both spouses being involved in an accident or having particularly unhealthy lifestyles.

At older ages, up to about 70 years, mortality rates of single people are usually the highest, although at the oldest ages, they appear to experience rather lower rates than other non-married groups. Thus the earlier findings that non-married people fare worse than married people remain, but the previously married do not appear to have higher mortality than the never-married (at least below about age 70). Results at the highest ages show a rather different pattern, but at these ages, there are issues with the accuracy of population data.[12]

These trends have been broadly stable over time, although there is some evidence of rising differentials between those married and those single, widowed or divorced.

Box 2

Measuring health in the Health Survey for England

'Health' (or its absence) may be defined and measured in many ways, the most common being self-reported morbidity and statistics produced by health services. Less frequently used are more detailed batteries of questions or physiological and laboratory-based measures, particularly for representative population samples. A recent study has shown that among older people, psychological aspects of health are more closely associated with marital status than self-reported morbidity.[44] The measures to be used here include self-reported measures of illness (limiting long-standing illness) and acute illness (in last two weeks), together with a question on general self-perceived health status. Psychological state has a major impact on overall health levels.

Two indicators of psychological wellbeing are used: responses to the General Health Questionnaire 12-scale (including questions about relationships, ability to concentrate and other issues), and a question on whether the person has any perceived lack of social support. Two objectively-measured indicators of health are whether or not a person is obese (BMI of over 30), and whether they are hypertensive (or are being treated for it). Finally, two health-related lifestyle indicators are whether the person smokes or not, and whether they exceed the recommended limits on alcohol consumption (14 units weekly for women, and 21 for men). In each case, the population was split into two groups, one with a good health indicator and one with a poor health indicator (Table 4.1).

Table **4.1**

Definition of alternative indicators of health

Indicator	Per cent	Sample size	Criterion
General Health Questionnaire	38.0	13,900	1 or more problems vs. none
Perceived lack of social support	37.6	13,940	Some vs. none
Body mass index	23.3	13,246	30 or over
Hypertensive	38.9	10,149	Blood pressure > 140 or treated hypertensive vs. others
Limiting long-standing illness	47.0	14,829	Limiting or non-limiting illness vs. none
Acute illness in last two weeks	17.2	14,825	Yes vs. no
General health	26.8	14,831	Fair', 'bad' or 'very bad' vs. 'good' or 'very good'
Alcohol consumption	23.2	14,813	Men > 21 units/week; women > 14 units
Cigarette smoker	25.2	14,808	Smoker vs. non-smoker
Total sample size		14,838	

Source: 2001 Health Survey for England (HSE)

Table **4.2**

Ratio of mortality rates by sex and age group of the single, widowed and divorced to that of married people (=100 for each age group), average over period 2002–2004

England and Wales

	30–34	35–39	40–44	45–49	50–54	55–59	60–64	65–69	70–74	75–79	80–84	85 and over
Males												
Single	252	280	289	270	246	235	216	184	158	144	115	99
Widowed	422	376	331	246	205	197	189	165	156	144	131	136
Divorced	231	232	244	235	220	198	188	169	157	145	128	125
Females												
Single	169	202	195	194	197	198	173	158	143	141	133	176
Widowed	260	256	203	208	182	162	156	149	144	134	129	164
Divorced	163	170	158	154	142	139	140	143	138	146	153	219

Source: Author's calculation using ONS data

Self-reported morbidity by marital status

Figure 4.3 shows the relationship between self-reported limiting long-term illness, age and marital status (from the 2001 Census of Great Britain). Although it is not a legal marital status, preliminary analysis showed that those classified as separated had similar patterns to the divorced. They have therefore been combined as a single group. Although these data refer to the whole population of Great Britain, the small numbers in some age groups can lead to unstable results, so the data have been smoothed.[45]

The results are broadly consistent with mortality data: young widowed people have much higher levels of limiting illness than their contemporaries, but the numbers involved are very small. Up to about age 75, the lowest rates are found among married people, and around age 40 they report only about half the level of the other groups. Around age 50, both single men and single women report the worst health, but from about age 80, they actually report the best health, with the worst health reported by widowed men and women. In particular, older single men report much lower rates than men in other marital status groups, and the increase with age is also much less.

The reasons for this cannot be established from these data. Older single men may form a particularly fit group (in part because they have been subject to higher mortality rates in earlier life and the more frail members may have already died), or their perceptions of what constitutes a limiting illness may differ from other groups. Nevertheless, this represents a change from 1991, when single people did not report such apparent health advantages at older ages.[18]

A complicating factor in the discussion of morbidity differentials is the role of institutionalisation. Married people are much less likely to be in a communal establishment at a given age (Table 4.4). For example, at ages 75–79, 1.0 per cent of married men are in an institution, compared with 9.8 per cent of single men. Since those in communal establishments are often there because of poor health, this will affect the distribution of ill health in the household sector. This is shown in Figure 4.5, where from around age 40, high proportions of those in communal establishments are in poor health, especially for single men and women.

By about age 75, around 95 per cent of those in communal establishments are reported as having poor health, whereas the figure among all marital status groups living in the community (private households) is much smaller. While non-married people report somewhat worse health than married people, it is implausible that the much higher rates of institutionalisation among the non-married, such as the 10-fold difference noted earlier, is a result solely of their substantially worse health. It is also likely to reflect the fact that many will not have a co-resident carer which would enable them to remain in the community.

One consequence of single people being more likely to enter institutions is that there is much less increase in reported prevalence of limiting long-standing illness with age among single men and women living in the community from about age 65 as compared with other marital status groups. This means that analyses based on household populations may provide potentially misleading information about overall trends in health by marital status at older ages.[18]

Figure **4.3**

Proportion with long-term illness by age and marital status, 2001

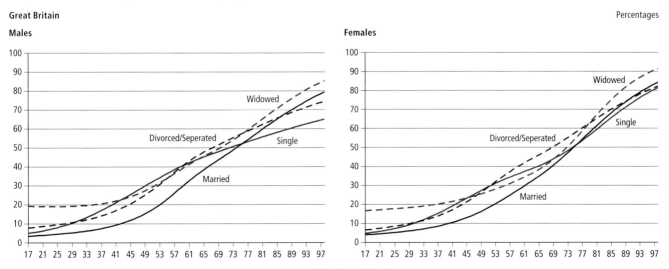

Source: 2001 Census, Office for National Statistics; General Register Office for Scotland

Considering the above, these data lend further support to Farr's conclusion that over the main age ranges, married people tend to have the best health.

Alternative measures of health

Mortality and self-reported morbidity, the two indicators discussed so far, are not the only measures of health. A series of alternative measures for the private household population in England can be considered. In this case, the numbers involved were such that only the overall summary measures of the relative risk associated with being in a particular marital status category were estimated.[46] Since marital, family characteristics and health all vary with age, age is controlled for in these analyses.[47] However, since the patterns of older and younger people were seen to be rather different (Figure 4.3), separate analyses were undertaken and presented for those aged 20 to 64, and 65 and over.

Table 4.6 shows on average the increased chance of being in the higher risk (poorer health) category after controlling for age, compared with the married group. (Table 4.6 shows data for four health indicators, data for five further health indicators are shown in the Appendix). The first point to note is that almost all of the values are greater than 1.0, (showing that the expected proportions are greater than for married people). For example, a separated man aged 20–64 is 50 per cent more

likely to report one or more psychological problems in the General Health Questions (GHQ) than a married man. Very few of the values below 1.0 are statistically significant.

These data also show those cohabiting. In most cases, the values for people in cohabiting couples are slightly higher than for married people, but the differentials are not large, (apart from the lifestyle indicators which may be partly because of the fact that they are less likely to have children present). The two objective indicators, BMI and hypertension (see Appendix), appear to show a different pattern, with the married population tending to be somewhat disadvantaged in many cases (although the differences are usually not statistically significant). While there is a general disadvantage among non-married groups, the divorced and separated tend to do rather worse than the other groups shown. Indeed, older single women have better health than married women on 7 of the 9 indicators (shown in Table 4.6 and in the Appendix), although older single men have worse health on 8 out of the 9 indicators compared with married older men, the main exception being BMI, which may reflect the generally poorer diet of non-married people.[48] In general, Farr's ranking of marital statuses seems to continue into the 21st Century at younger ages, with the previously married doing worst, but with older single people living in the community having relatively good health.

Table **4.4**

Proportion of people in communal establishments by age, sex and marital status, 2001

Great Britain

Percentages

	Males					Females			
Age group	Single	Married	Widowed	Div/Sep[1]		Single	Married	Widowed	Div/Sep[1]
17–19	7.7	3.0	5.1	4.1		7.2	0.6	3.3	2.2
20–24	5.7	1.4	5.2	6.1		4.4	0.4	4.9	1.2
25–29	2.6	0.6	5.1	3.8		1.5	0.2	2.3	0.6
30–34	2.1	0.4	3.5	2.1		1.0	0.1	1.9	0.4
35–39	2.2	0.2	2.1	1.6		1.2	0.1	0.8	0.3
40–44	2.5	0.2	1.5	1.2		1.7	0.1	0.6	0.3
45-49	2.9	0.2	1.0	1.0		2.5	0.1	0.5	0.3
50–54	3.6	0.2	0.9	1.0		3.5	0.1	0.4	0.4
55–59	4.3	0.2	0.8	1.3		4.5	0.1	0.5	0.5
60–64	4.6	0.2	1.0	1.4		4.8	0.1	0.6	0.7
65–69	5.3	0.2	1.4	1.8		4.9	0.2	0.9	1.0
70–74	6.8	0.4	2.5	2.7		6.0	0.5	1.9	1.7
75–79	9.8	1.0	4.2	4.6		8.5	1.3	4.2	3.0
80–84	11.8	2.2	7.2	6.8		13.6	3.2	8.8	5.3
85–89	20.7	5.0	13.2	12.6		24.1	8.5	17.5	10.2
90 & over	22.2	10.8	24.8	15.6		40.6	18.3	34.7	18.5

1 Divorced or separated.

Source: 2001 Census, Office for National Statistics; General Register Office for Scotland

Figure **4.5**

Proportion with long-term illness in private households: by marital status and age, 2001

Great Britain   Percentages

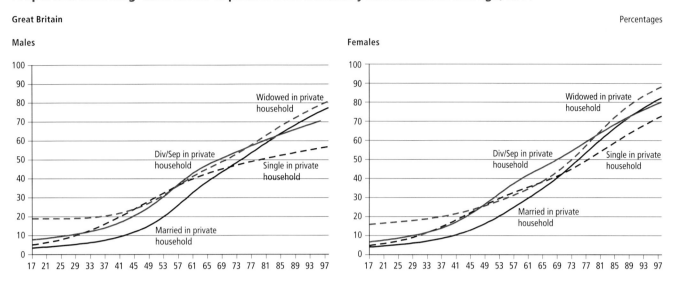

Proportion with long-term illness in communal establishments: by marital status and age, 2001

Great Britain   Percentages

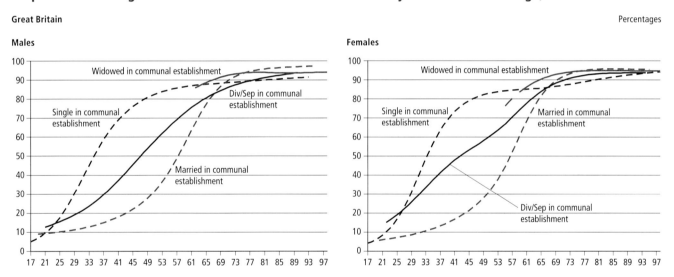

Source: 2001 Census, Office for National Statistics; General Register Office for Scotland

Morbidity by family status

The relationship between mortality and family status has been studied less extensively than marital status, largely because suitable data are not readily available. However, family arrangements are related to health status. As above, the 2001 Census of Great Britain and 2001 HSE are used to investigate how living arrangements are related to health status.

Figure 4.7 shows the proportion of individuals with a limiting long-term illness by family type, and is based on data from the 2001 Census. The population is classified as to whether a person is a member of a couple, married or cohabiting and with or without children. The other groups are lone parents, living as a child in a family unit, or not living as part of a family. As noted

above, the direction of causality is not clear. People's living arrangements may be a consequence of their health status, such as when frail elderly persons move in with their children.

There is also the question of who is providing assistance. The fact that people around age 40 who are living with their parents(s) and not in a partnership show the highest levels of ill health suggests that some may require family support. However, the proportion of females with poor health who are a child in the family remains almost constant from about age 45 (the numbers above age 75 are insufficient for analysis).

Among adults between ages 30 and 65, those not living as part of a family unit also show high rates of illness. For those living as a couple, the difference between being married or

Table **4.6**

Relative risk of health problem by marital status (married = 1), by age and sex, 2001

England

	Age group 20–64		Age group 65 and over	
	Men	Women	Men	Women
General Health Questionnaire (GHQ)				
Single	1.14*	1.22*	1.44*	1.04
Separated	1.50*	1.58*	1.02	1.63*
Divorced	1.32*	1.26*	1.68*	1.17
Widowed	1.02	1.30*	1.16	1.06
Cohabiting	1.10	1.14*	0.85	1.55*
Body mass index				
Single	0.85	0.92	0.93	0.71
Separated	0.87	1.00	1.06	0.34
Divorced	0.92	0.97	0.69	1.09
Widowed	1.04	1.06	1.00	0.93
Cohabiting	1.07	0.89	0.80	1.45
Limiting long-standing illness				
Single	1.15*	1.24*	1.09	0.87
Separated	1.11	1.34*	1.10	1.03
Divorced	1.26*	1.27*	1.01	1.10
Widowed	0.96	1.18*	1.01	1.01
Cohabiting	1.12	1.07	0.61*	0.95
Cigarette smoker				
Single	1.32*	1.75*	2.29*	0.84
Separated	1.43*	1.66*	1.49	2.56*
Divorced	1.79*	1.99*	2.41*	1.14
Widowed	1.27	1.67*	2.05*	1.45*
Cohabiting	1.44*	1.66*	2.03	1.42

Note: The * shows results that are statistically significant (different from 1.0 at 5% level). Models control for age by including linear and quadratic age terms (not shown).

Source: 2001 HSE

cohabiting is very small, and in both cases, those with children tend to report rather better health. However, lone parents stand out as having the highest rates of long standing illness, reporting worse health than two-parent families with children, with the differential being particularly pronounced for working-age male lone parents. The high levels found among lone parents persist up to the oldest ages, although the reasons for this may change, as noted previously.

These findings are consistent with earlier findings that better health is associated with having children living in the family as long as both parents are present. Being a lone parent, however, is associated with poorer health.

For England, alternative indicators by family type are available from the 2001 HSE. In this case, four groups are distinguished, with and without a partner, and with or without a child in the household. The estimates of relative risk are calculated with reference to those with a partner but no child (Table 4.8, with further data shown in the Appendix). Differences among couples aged under 65 with a child are small. Those with a child tend to be slightly better on the majority of indicators. Those without a partner, irrespective of whether they have a child or not, do worse on most indicators (apart for BMI and hypertension). The disadvantages of these non-partnered groups are larger on the psychological measures of social support and GHQ, and this contributes to the poorer scores on the general health question. Among older people, there is a divergence, with women tending to receive less benefit from partnership (which is overwhelmingly marriage at these ages) than men.

Figure **4.7**

Proportion with long-term illness by age and family type, 2001

Great Britain

Males

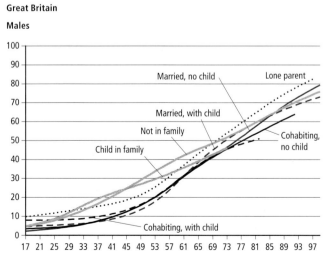

Females

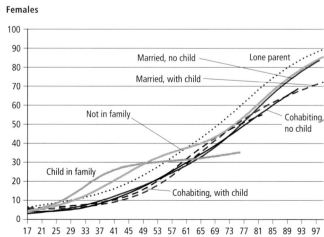

Source: 2001 Census, Office for National Statistics; General Register Office for Scotland

Table 4.8

Relative risk of health problem by family type (with partner and no child(ren) = 1), by age and sex, 2001

England

	Age group 20–64		Age group 65 and over	
	Men	Women	Men	Women
General Health Questionnaire				
No partner, no child	1.17*	1.25*	1.30*	1.07
No partner, child	1.15	1.22*	1.69*	1.11
Partner & child	0.98	0.99	1.28	0.99
Body mass index				
No partner, no child	0.83*	1.03	0.99	0.86
No partner, child	0.82	1.07	0.94	1.10
Partner & child	0.93	1.13	1.52*	0.83
Limiting long-standing illness				
No partner, no child	1.16*	1.19*	1.05	1.00
No partner, child	1.14	1.12*	0.94	1.03
Partner & child	1.03	0.89*	0.97	1.01
Cigarette smoker				
No partner, no child	1.22*	1.34*	2.19*	1.39*
No partner, child	1.46*	1.92*	1.59	1.20
Partner & child	0.95	1.02	1.34	1.09

Note: The * shows results that are statistically significant (different from 1.0 at 5% level). Models control for age by including linear and quadratic age terms (not shown)

Source: 2001 HSE

Again, many of these findings are consistent with earlier results and those from other industrialised countries.

Morbidity of children by family status

Infant mortality shows substantial differences by social class, but births for which no father is recorded on the birth certificate (which means that information on the father's social class is unavailable), have the highest rates of all.[35] With increasing patterns of partnership breakdown and re-partnering, many children will spend time with only one parent, or with step-parents: even if they are with both natural parents, they may have stepsiblings from a parent's previous relationships. In the 2001 Census, the large numbers and detailed information on relationships of household members means that it is possible to analyse such families in more detail than before.

Almost two thirds of children under 16 were living with both natural parents and no stepsiblings, about one in five lived with a lone mother and the rest in a variety of parental arrangements (Table 4.9). The group: 'natural parents and

Table 4.9

Relative risk of limiting long-term illness among children 0–15 by family type (with both natural parents = 1), by age and sex, 2001

Great Britain

Family type	Relative risk	Number	Distribution per cent
Both natural parents	1.00	8,285,403	65.0
Natural mother and stepfather	1.30	464,577	3.6
Natural father and stepmother	1.11	58,043	0.5
Natural parents and stepfather	1.32	658,157	5.2
Natural parents and stepmother	1.27	113,388	0.9
Stepmother and stepfather	1.18	60,617	0.5
Natural parents and stepmother and stepfather	1.34	21,904	0.2
Lone mother	1.66	2,684,767	21.1
Lone father	1.29	255,918	2.0
Not in a family	1.87	135,155	1.1
Total		12,737,929	100

Note: All relative risk values are statistically significant (different from 1.0 at 5% level). Models control for age by including linear and quadratic age terms (not shown).

Source: 2001 Census, Office for National Statistics; General Register Office for Scotland

stepmother and stepfather' is a family unit where there are natural children of both partners, and each partner also has one or more children by another partner. In total, about one in ten children live in a family unit that contains some children that are not the natural children of the male partner.

Table 4.9 shows the relative risks of a child being reported as having a long-standing illness compared with those in families that contain only the natural children of the partners. Children in all other family types have values above one, showing they are more likely to have a long-standing illness. The highest values are those not in a family, but the next highest group, with chance of illness about two thirds higher than the reference group, is children living with a lone mother (as also found in the HSE analysis). The excess risk of other family types shown in Table 4.9 is generally about 30 per cent higher than for the reference group.

As with all these findings, care should be taken about attributing causality. Children whose parents experience partnership breakdown do not increase their chance of ill health by two thirds as a consequence. The only meaningful comparison is with what would have happened if the breakdown had not occurred. By definition, this is unknown. In addition, there may be more scrutiny of lone parent or step-parent families so that children are more likely to be diagnosed with a particular condition.[49] It seems once more that the comments of William Farr are as pertinent today as when he wrote in 1861 'We do not want impressions, we want facts ... I must repeat my objections to intermingling Causation with Statistics ... The statistician has nothing to do with causation; he is almost certain in the present state of knowledge to err.'[50]

Explanations for the observed relationships: selection, protection and stress effects

Three main theories have been advanced to account for variations in health status by marital and family status.

Selection effects

The first of these is concerned with selection effects: chronically ill people are less likely to marry and remain married and thus enjoy the instrumental and emotional benefits of a stable marriage, which tend to maintain good health. Younger ill adults may be less able to leave the parental home and also less likely to have children. At the upper end of the age range, illness may lead to them moving in with relatives or friends. Unhealthy individuals are thought to be less likely to marry or stay married because ill health is seen to interfere with establishing and maintaining relationships.[51]

In a British study of a cohort born in 1946, a significant proportion of persons who were still single in their mid-30s had received special education as children.[52] Evidence on mortality differentials among those under age 65 from a number of countries also lends support to the selection argument. One study has shown that the smaller the proportion of the population in the non-married groups, the greater their excess risk.[53] Selection effects may also influence the health status of the divorced, widowed, and remarried populations because those who remarry may be healthier than those who remain widowed or divorced.[54]

Of course, different selection processes may affect the composition of different marital status groups at different ages. Young people who remain single may be conforming to Western societal norms that discourage very early marriage, whereas older single people have **not** conformed to the norm of eventual marriage.[26] As such, there is some evidence that for younger marriages the selection effect acts so that those who marry young have less favourable health characteristics than the unmarried, where the reverse is true for those who marry later.[55] Those who marry young are more likely to have children.[56] Those who are widowed, especially at relatively young ages, may also share various characteristics with their deceased spouse, including a

common environment, and so themselves be selected for poor health; additionally the stress of bereavement or marital breakdown may itself have negative consequences for health.[57]

Most studies have found that relationships between indicators of health and marital status are weaker in older age groups. In fact, one study found that at older ages never-married women had better health outcomes than their married counterparts.[17] There is considerable evidence to indicate that increase in disability among older people leads to changes in their living arrangements, particularly resulting in moves to institutions or the households of relatives.[58] The health status, and subsequent mortality, of individuals making these kinds of household transitions has been shown to be much worse than that of other elderly people.[59]

Protective effects

The second set of explanations for marital status differentials in health focuses on the protective effects of marriage. Marriage is hypothesised to confer health benefits through the provision of emotional and social support,[60] which may act as a buffer against the potentially harmful effects of stress.[61] Spouses, particularly wives, may discourage unhealthy and promote healthy life styles, for example, decreases in smoking.[22] There has been increasing support for the theory that part of the health protective effects of marriage are economic in nature.[14] Another advantage of marriage is the availability of a regular sex partner.[62] Marriage is also strongly associated with living arrangements, which may themselves influence health. For example, some studies suggest that older men who live alone have poorer morale and a poorer diet than those living with a spouse or with others.[63]

Although sometimes advanced as competing hypotheses, both selective and protective effects are likely to be important and to reinforce each other, in that the more advantaged tend to marry and to obtain the protective benefits of marriage. Finally, marriage may also bring control of unhealthy behaviours. For example, unmarried men have higher rates of alcohol consumption than married men.[22] Married people are in general financially better-off than non-married, which will also tend to reinforce the advantages of this state.

There is clear evidence of the protective effect of marriage over and above selection effects. At the same time, there is a considerable debate as to the relative contribution of social and economic aspects of marriage to the positive association between marriage and health. The social and psychological benefits of marriage include social interaction, intimacy, companionship and support, all of which are assumed to decrease morbidity and mortality. In particular, married women are likely to promote the health of others within the household by encouraging healthier behaviour such as healthier eating habits and visiting the doctor. Married men are thought to avoid risky behaviour and consequently conduct healthier lifestyles.[22] As married people, especially women, are generally financially better off than their unmarried counterparts, marriage's beneficial effects on health may be caused by these individuals' greater access to resources. The US Panel Study of Income Dynamics has been used to show that once poverty status was controlled for, none of the marital status variables for women were significant.[28]

Stress of bereavement or marital breakdown

The third hypothesised explanation for variations in health status between currently and formerly married individuals is that the stress of bereavement, or marital breakdown, has negative consequences for health. The stress of a transition to widowhood (or the divorced state) has adverse health consequences, which may be compounded by effects associated both with the state of being widowed, such as the loss of support, as well as with the event of widowhood.[64]

Conclusion

The health benefits associated with partnership, especially marriage, have been recognised since the 19th Century. Changing social and economic trends might have been expected to attenuate these benefits. Formerly, marriage was highly prized (even if high proportions were unable to marry in earlier centuries), but increasingly those with the widest choices in society are opting to delay or finding alternatives to marriage. In the past, some behaviours were frowned upon, such as divorce or extra-marital childbearing, but are now much more common. It might be expected that as the stigma attached to such behaviours declines, so should any health penalty associated with them. Former benefits of partnership, such as a generally better standard of living, seem less important as the single breadwinner model disappears. For a number of reasons, differences between marital status groups might be expected to decline, but the clearest evidence (given by mortality trends) suggests that these differentials are, in fact, increasing, so that the link between health and family remains strong.

Acknowledgements

Thanks are due to the Office for National Statistics for unpublished tabulations and to members of staff, especially Hannah McConnell, Steve Smallwood and Ben Wilson, for assistance and comments on this chapter. Any mistakes remain the responsibility of the author.

Notes and references

1   Despite this, the fact that one's family extends beyond the confines of the household is sometimes ignored, see Grundy E, Murphy M and Shelton N (1999) 'Looking beyond the household: inter-generational perspectives on living kin and contacts with kin in Great Britain', *Population Trends* 97, pp 19–27.

2   Bowling A (1995) *Measuring Disease: a review of Disease-specific Quality of Life Measurement Scales*, Open University Press: Buckingham.

3   World Health Organization (1948) *Official Records of the World Health Organization* No 2, World Health Organization: Geneva.

4   WHOQOL Group (1993) *Measuring Quality of Life: the Development of the World Health Organization Quality of Life Instrument* (WHOQOL), World Health Organization: Geneva.

5   Diener, E, Gohm CL, Suh E, and Oishi S (2000) 'Similarity of the relations between marital status and subjective well-being across cultures', *Journal of Cross-Cultural Psychology* 31(4), pp 419–436.

6   Farr W (1858) 'The influence of marriage on the mortality of the French people', *Transactions of the National Association for the Promotion of Social Science*, 504–512. (Reprinted in *Vital Statistics: A Memorial Volume of Selections from the Reports and Writings of William Farr,* (1975) The Library of the New York Academy of Medicine – The Scarecrow Press: Metuchen, NJ, pp 438–441.)

7   For example: Van Poppel F and Joung I (2001) 'Long-Term Trends in Marital Status Mortality Differences in The Netherlands 1850–1970', *Journal of Biosocial Science* 33, pp 279–303.

8   For example: Prior PM and Hayes BC (2003) 'The relationship between marital status and health: an empirical investigation of differences in bed occupancy within health and social care facilities in Britain, 1921–1991', *Journal of Family Issues* 24 (1), pp 124–148.

9   For example: Kiecolt-Glaser JK, Kennedy S, Malkoff S, Fisher L, Speicher CE and Glaser R (1988) 'Marital discord and immunity in males', *Psychosomatic Medicine* 50, pp 213–229.

10 Lillard LA and Waite LJ (1995) '"Till death do us part": Marital disruption and mortality', *American Journal of Sociology* 100, pp 1131–1156.

11 Valkonen T, Martikainen P and Blomgren J (2004) *Increasing excess mortality among non-married elderly people in developed countries*, Demographic Research Special Collection 2, Article 12, available at: www.demographic-research.org

12 Murphy M, Grundy E, and Kalogirou S (2007, forthcoming) 'The increase in marital-status differences in mortality up to the oldest age in seven European countries, 1990–99', *Population Studies*.

13 Martikainen P, Martelin T, Nihtila E, Majamaa K and Koskinen S (2005) 'Differences in mortality by marital status in Finland from 1976 to 2000: Analyses of changes in marital-status distributions, socio-demographic and household composition, and cause of death', *Population Studies* 59, pp 99–115.

14 For example: Hahn BA (1993) 'Marital status and women's health – the effect of economic marital acquisitions', *Journal of Marriage and the Family* 55, pp 495–504.

15 Adelmann PK, Antonucci TC, Crohan SE and Coleman LM (1990) 'A Causal Analysis of Employment and Health in Midlife Women', *Women and Health* 16, pp 5–17.

16 Litwak E and Messeri P (1989) 'Organizational theory, social supports, and mortality rates: a theoretical convergence', *American Sociological Review* 54, pp 49–66.

17 Goldman N, Korenman S and Weinstein R (1995) 'Marital status and health among the elderly', *Social Science and Medicine* 40, pp 1717–1730.

18 For example: Glaser K, Murphy M and Grundy E (1997) 'Limiting long-term illness and household structure among people aged 45 and over, Great Britain 1991', *Ageing and Society* 17, pp 3–19.

19 Waite LJ and Gallagher M (2000) *The case for marriage: why married people are happier, healthier, and better off financially*, Doubleday : New York.

20 For example: McEwen BS and Stellar E (1993) 'Stress and the Individual: Mechanisms leading to disease', *Archives of Internal Medicine* 153, pp 2093–2101.

21 For example: Murphy M, Glaser K and Grundy E (1997) 'Marital status and long-term illness in Great Britain', *Journal of Marriage and the Family* 59, pp 156–164.

22 Umberson D (1992) 'Gender, marital status and the social control of health behavior', *Social Science and Medicine* 34, pp 907–917.

23 ONS Longitudinal Study, based on one per cent of the population enumerated in the 1971 Census.

24 Fox AJ and Goldblatt PO (1982) 'Longitudinal Study: socio demographic mortality differentials', *LS Series* No 1. HMSO: London.

25 Grundy EMD (1992) 'Socio-demographic variations in rates of movement into institutions among elderly people in England and Wales: an analysis of linked census and mortality data 1971–1985', *Population Studies* 46, pp 65–84.

26 Murphy M and Sullivan O (1986) 'Unemployment, housing and household structure among young adults', *Journal of Social Policy* 15, pp 205–222.

27 Verbrugge L (1989) 'The twain meet: Empirical explanations of sex differences in health and mortality', *Journal of Health and Social Behaviour* 30, pp 282–304.

28 Zick CD and Smith KR (1991) 'Marital transitions, poverty, and gender differences in mortality', *Journal of Marriage and the Family* 53, pp 327–336.

29 Wickrama KA, Lorenz FO, Conger RD, Elder GH Jr., Todd AW and Fang SA (2006) 'Changes in family financial circumstances and the physical health of married and recently divorced mothers', *Social Science and Medicine* 63 (1), pp 123–36.

30 For example: Willitts M, Benzeval M and Stansfeld S (2004) 'Partnership history and mental health over time', *Journal of Epidemiology and Community Health* 58, pp 53–58.

31 Clausen JA (1987) 'Health and the Life Course: Some Personal Observations', J*ournal of Health and Social Behavior* 28, pp 337–344.

32 For example: Cherlin AJP, Chase-Lansdale L and McRae C (1998) 'Effects of Parental Divorce on Mental Health Throughout the Life Course', *American Sociological Review* 63 (2), pp 239–249.

33 For example: Rodgers B and Pryor J (1998) 'Divorce and separation: the outcomes for children', Joseph Rowntree Foundation: York.

34 Angel R and Worobey JL (1985) 'Single Motherhood and Children's Health', *Journal of Health and Social Behavior* 29, pp 38–52.

35 Office for National Statistics (2006) 'Infant and Perinatal Mortality by Social and Biological Factors, 2005', *Health Statistics Quarterly* 32, pp 82–86.

36 Corbin T (2005) 'Investigation into sudden infant death and unascertained infant deaths in England and Wales, 1995–2003' (Table 8), *Health Statistics Quarterly* 27, pp 17–23.

37 Kleinman JC and Kessel SS (1987) 'Racial Differences in Low Birth Weight', *New England Journal of Medicine* 317, pp 749–753.

38 Umberson D (1987) 'Family Status and Health Behaviors: Social Control as a Dimension of Social Integration', *Journal of Health and Social Behavior* 28, pp 309–316.

39 For example: Idler EL and Kasl S (1991) 'Health perceptions and survival: Do global evaluations of health status really predict mortality?', *Journal of Gerontology* 46, pp S55–S65.

40 Sadana R, Mathers CD, Lopez AD, Murray CJL and Iburg KM (2002) 'Comparative analyses of more than 50 household surveys on health status', Chapter 8.1 in Murray CJL, Salomon JA, Mathers CD and Lopez AD (eds) *Summary Measures of Population Health Concepts, Ethics, Measurement and Applications*, World Health Organization: Geneva, pp 369–386.

41 Walker A, O'Brien M, Traynor J, Fox K, Goddard E, and Foster K (2002) *Living in Britain: Results from the 2001 General Household Survey*, Table 7.1, TSO: London.

42 Bennett N, Dodd T, Flatley J, Freeth S, and Bolling K (1995) *Health Survey for England 1993*, HMSO: London.

43 Murray CJL and Lopez AD (1996) *The global burden of disease: a comprehensive assessment of mortality and disability from diseases, injuries, and risk factors in 1990 and projected to 2020*, Harvard University Press: Cambridge, MA.

44 Grundy E and Sloggett A (2003) 'Health inequalities in the older population: the role of personal capital, social resources and socio-economic circumstances', *Social Science and Medicine* 56 (5), pp 935–47.

45 Smoothing was carried out using a series of Generalised Additive Models (GAMs) – see Hastie T and Tibsharani R (1990) *Generalised Additive Models*, Chapman and Hall: London. The GAM model is based on an iterative scatterplot smoothing algorithm, which obtains a preliminary smoothed value and uses this value to fit the model to obtain a better value, until the model converges to a smooth value with optimal statistical properties.

46 Calculated using the method in Zou G (2004) 'A Modified Poisson Regression Approach to Prospective Studies with Binary Data', *American Journal of Epidemiology* 159 (7), pp 702–6.

47 Age has been included in linear and quadratic form.

48 Davis MA, Murphy SP, Neuhaus JM and Lein D (1990) 'Living arrangements and dietary quality of older U.S. adults', *Journal of the American Dietetic Association* 90, pp 1667–1672.

49 Macintyre S (1992) 'The effects of family position and status on health', *Social Science and Medicine* 35, pp 453–464.

50 Cited in Diamond M and Stone M (1981) 'Nightingale on Quetelet', *Journal of the Royal Statistical Society: Series A* 144, pp 70.

51 Brown JS and Giesy B (1986) 'Marital status of persons with spinal cord injury', *Social Science and Medicine* 23, pp 313–322.

52 Kiernan K (1988) 'Who remains celibate?' *Journal of Biosocial Science* 20, pp 253–263.

53 Hu Y and Goldman N (1990) 'Mortality Differentials by Marital Status: An International Comparison', *Demography* 27, pp 233–250.

54 Helsing, KJ, Szklo M and Comstock GW (1981) 'Factors associated with mortality after widowhood', *American Journal of Public Health* 71, pp 802–809.

55 For example: Cheung YB and Sloggett A (1998) 'Health and adverse selection into marriage: evidence from a study of the 1958 British birth cohort', *Public Health* 112 (5), pp 309–11.

56 Office of Population Censuses and Surveys (1983) 'Fertility report from the 1971 census: the Registrar General's decennial supplement for England and Wales 1971', *Series DS* no.5. HMSO: London.

57 Bowling A (1994) 'Mortality after bereavement: An analysis of mortality rates and associations with mortality 13 years after bereavement', *International Journal of Geriatric Psychiatry* 9, pp 445–59.

58 For example: Grundy E and Glaser K (1997) 'Trends in, and transitions to, institutional residence among older people in England and Wales, 1971 to 1991', *Journal of Epidemiology and Community Health* 51, pp 531–540.

59 For example: Glaser K and Grundy E (1998) 'Migration and household change in the population aged 65 and over, 1971–1991', *International Journal of Population Geography* 4, pp 323–339.

60 Wyke S and Ford G (1992) 'Competing explanations for associations between marital status and health', *Social Science and Medicine* 34, pp 523–532.

61 Berkman LF (1988) 'The changing and heterogeneous nature of aging and longevity: A social and biomedical perspective', *Annual Reviews in Gerontology and Geriatrics* 8, pp 37–68.

62 Waite LJ (1995) 'Does marriage matter?', *Demography* 32, pp 483–507.

63 For example: Cox BD, Blaxter M, Buckle ALJ, Fenner WP, Golding JF and Gore M (1987) *The health and lifestyle survey*, Health Promotion Research Trust: London.

64 For example: Jones DR, Goldblatt P.O and Leon D (1984) 'Bereavement and cancer: Some data on deaths of spouses from the longitudinal study of OPCS', *British Medical Journal* 289, pp 700–702.

Family geography

Ben Wilson and Steve Smallwood

Chapter 5

Introduction

This chapter investigates the geographical differences between families and family types. Although the geographical differences between families are of interest in their own right, the chapter can also be used in conjunction with the previous chapters in this volume to understand other family variations. The three topics covered so far in this volume – health, education and unpaid care – show variation according to geography. Given the associations we have seen with family type, these variations will, at least in part, be a reflection of the geographical variations in family types.

Although ONS regularly publishes population information at sub-national levels,[1] there is insufficient information on how the population changes over time to create sub-national population figures by marital status or by family type. Surveys, the alternative source of population numbers at one point in time, are often hampered by small sample sizes at the sub-national level. The census is therefore the best source for geographical analysis of the family.

Further, as discussed in previous chapters, the 2001 Census provides the most detailed family information of any UK census. In particular, the inclusion of a relationship matrix allows complex family types and multigenerational families to be identified and

analysed. The increasing variety of modern families, in part caused by cohabitation, divorce and re-partnering, has been identified previously (see Chapter 1). It is important that this complexity is captured by data sources, and as such, the 2001 Census should be considered a success. Furthermore, the Census provides a reliable picture of geographical differences, particularly at higher levels of geography such as:

- GOR   Government Office Region

- LAD   Local Authority District (England and Wales)

- DCA   District Council Area (Northern Ireland)

- SCA   Scottish Council Area (Scotland)

Maps

This chapter features a number of maps that aim to communicate geographical results in the most appropriate and effective way. A consistent method has been used throughout to decide how maps should be shaded, with the data being sorted into five quantiles (categories), each containing one-fifth of the values. Each section of the map is then shaded according to the category of its data.

Each category has the same number of values. For example, the first category contains the lowest 20 per cent of values.

Table 5.1

Proportion of families by type for each region (country or Government Office Region), 2001

United Kingdom

Percentages

	Lone parent family (male)	Lone parent family (female)	Married couple non-stepfamily[1]	Married couple stepfamily[2]	Cohabiting couple non-stepfamily[1]	Cohabiting couple stepfamily[2]
UK	2.2	14.2	67.3	3.0	11.0	2.3
North East	2.2	15.8	66.3	3.2	10.0	2.6
North West	2.4	16.3	65.2	3.2	10.3	2.5
Yorkshire and The Humber	2.1	13.6	67.0	3.4	11.2	2.7
East Midlands	2.1	12.0	68.8	3.3	11.2	2.6
West Midlands	2.4	14.0	67.9	3.2	10.2	2.3
East	2.0	10.9	70.2	3.1	11.4	2.4
London	2.7	19.5	59.3	2.6	14.3	1.7
South East	1.9	11.1	69.9	3.1	11.7	2.3
South West	1.9	11.3	70.1	3.3	11.1	2.3
Wales/Cymru	2.4	15.1	67.4	3.2	9.7	2.2
Scotland	2.4	15.9	67.8	2.4	9.4	2.1
Northern Ireland	2.6	18.0	71.2	2.1	5.0	1.1

Note: Percentages may not add up because of rounding
1 Non-stepfamilies include families without children
2 Stepchildren may be dependent or non-dependent

Source: 2001 Census, Office for National Statistics; General Register Office for Scotland; Northern Ireland Statistics and Research Agency

Although a different method could have been used to categorise the data, quantiles were chosen because they are less susceptible to extreme values.[2] Other methods may give a greater visual impression of the differences between values, for instance, but in some cases this may actually exaggerate differences. Generally, the quantile method is the most intuitive and leads to the greatest understanding of the data, not only for individual maps, but also where two or more maps are compared.

Families in the UK

Table 1.3 in Chapter One provides an overview of the numbers of families by type for the constituent countries of the UK in 2001. In this chapter, Table 5.1 shows the proportion of families by type for each Country or Government Office Region. These tables can be used to compare with results at different levels of geography that are presented in this chapter.

Approximately 70 per cent of families in the UK in 2001 were married couple families. Of the remainder, around 13 per cent were cohabiting couple families and 16 per cent were lone parents. By comparison, the results for 1991 for Great Britain were: 79 per cent married, 8 per cent cohabiting and 13 per cent lone parents. As such, it appears that the largest change in recent years has been the decrease in married families, with a corresponding increase in the other family types, cohabiting and lone parents.

Family type by country and GOR

Map 5.2 displays a summary of families by Country and GOR, and is based on the figures provided in Table 5.1. The South East had the largest number of families, 2,279,275; Northern Ireland had the smallest, 442,584. Notable variations in families by region are:

Lone Parents

In 2001, 22.1 per cent of families in London were lone parent families, the largest proportion for any region. After London, the North East, North West, Wales, Scotland and Northern Ireland all had a greater than average proportion of lone parent families. The smallest proportions of lone parent families were in the East, South East and South West, each with approximately 13 per cent.

The great majority of lone parent families were female. London had the largest proportion of male lone parent families, 2.7 per cent while the proportion ranged between 1.9 and 2.6 per cent for other regions.

Stepfamilies

The number of stepfamilies was reasonably consistent across regions, with the exception of London, Scotland and Northern Ireland. Yorkshire and the Humber had the highest proportion of married stepfamilies, 3.4 per cent. For cohabiting stepfamilies, all regions were closely clustered around the average proportion for the UK, 2.3 per cent. The exception was Northern Ireland with only 1.1 per cent, reflecting the low levels of cohabitation in Northern Ireland overall.

Married

In the UK, 67.3 per cent of families were married couples that were not a stepfamily. However in the East, South West and Northern Ireland, over 70 per cent of families were married and not stepfamilies. London had the smallest proportion of married families that were not stepfamilies, only 59.3 per cent. It also had the smallest proportion of married families (of all types), 61.9 per cent.

Cohabitation

In London, 14.3 per cent of families were cohabiting non-stepfamilies. This figure was the largest proportion for any region, and noticeably different from the average 11.0 per cent. Also noticeably different from the average, Northern Ireland was the region with the smallest proportion of cohabiting families that were not stepfamilies, 5.0 per cent. Scotland and Wales also had smaller than average proportions of cohabiting non-stepfamilies families, 9.4 and 9.7 per cent respectively.

Children in families

There are three main types of child status used to classify families. These are:

1. no children

2. dependent children

3. non-dependent children only

It is important to note that a family classified as with 'dependent children', may actually contain non-dependent children as well. In other words, a family that has both dependent and non-dependent children is classified as a dependent child family. Usually, dependent child families are further split into those with one, two and three or more dependent children, but they may contain more children than this including non-dependent children.

Map 5.3 shows the proportion of families for each region according to their child status (for the numerical results please see the Appendix). In 2001 in the UK, 41.6 per cent of families had no children. In London, the equivalent figure was only 35.9 per cent, but in Northern Ireland it was even lower, 28.7 per cent. The South West had the largest proportion of families with no children, 46.9 per cent.

In general, regions with a lower than average proportion of families with no children had a higher than average proportion of families with non-dependent children. The South West had

Map **5.2**

Lone parent families[1]: by country or region, 2001

United Kingdom

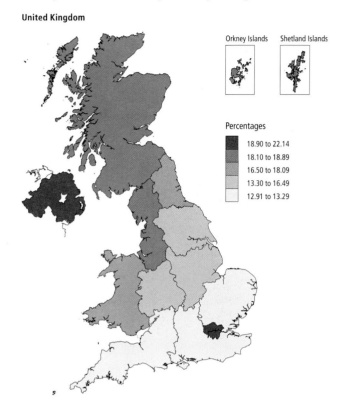

Orkney Islands   Shetland Islands

Percentages

- 18.90 to 22.14
- 18.10 to 18.89
- 16.50 to 18.09
- 13.30 to 16.49
- 12.91 to 13.29

Stepfamilies[1]: by country or region, 2001

United Kingdom

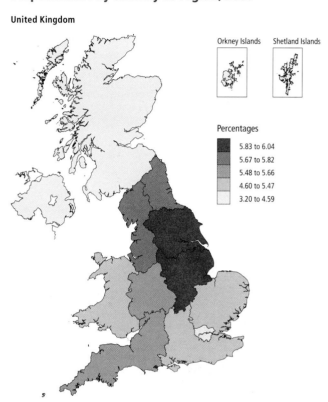

Orkney Islands   Shetland Islands

Percentages

- 5.83 to 6.04
- 5.67 to 5.82
- 5.48 to 5.66
- 4.60 to 5.47
- 3.20 to 4.59

Married couple families[1]: by country or region, 2001

United Kingdom

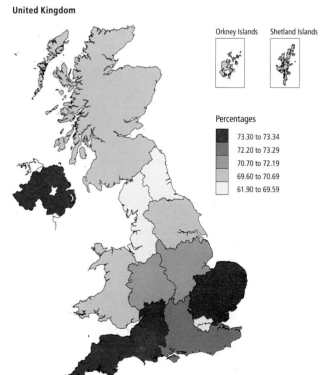

Orkney Islands   Shetland Islands

Percentages

- 73.30 to 73.34
- 72.20 to 73.29
- 70.70 to 72.19
- 69.60 to 70.69
- 61.90 to 69.59

Cohabiting couple families[1]: by country or region, 2001

United Kingdom

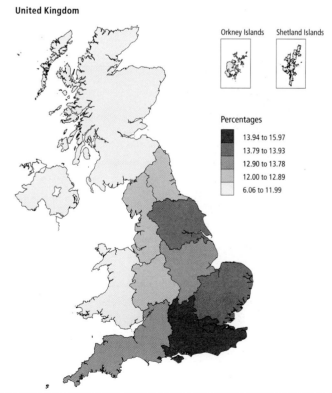

Orkney Islands   Shetland Islands

Percentages

- 13.94 to 15.97
- 13.79 to 13.93
- 12.90 to 13.78
- 12.00 to 12.89
- 6.06 to 11.99

1   As a proportion of all families in each region.

Source: 2001 Census, Office for National Statistics; General Register Office for Scotland; Northern Ireland Statistics and Research Agency

Map **5.3**

Families with no children[1]: by country or region, 2001

United Kingdom

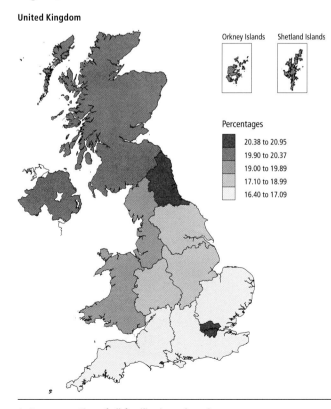

Families with non-dependent children only[1]: by country or region, 2001

United Kingdom

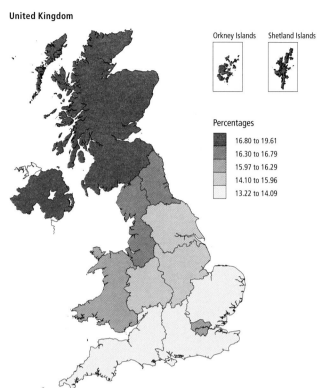

Families with one dependent child[1]: by country or region, 2001

United Kingdom

Families with three or more dependent children[1]: by country or region, 2001

United Kingdom

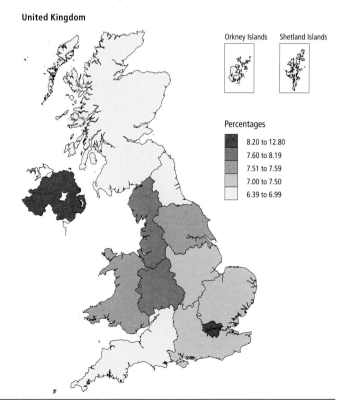

1 As a proportion of all families in each region.

Source: 2001 Census, Office for National Statistics; General Register Office for Scotland; Northern Ireland Statistics and Research Agency

the smallest proportion of families with non-dependent children, 13.2 per cent, while Northern Ireland had the largest, 19.6 per cent.

London had the largest proportion of families with one dependent child, 21.0 per cent. Similarly, the equivalent percentages for the North East, Scotland and Northern Ireland were all larger than 20 per cent. Excluding London, the southern regions had a smaller proportion of families with one dependent child compared with the northern regions.

The regions that had the greatest proportion of large dependent families (three or more dependent children) were Northern Ireland with 12.8 per cent, London with 9.3 per cent, West Midlands with 8.1 per cent and the North West with 7.9 per cent. This is in contrast to Scotland, the North East and South West, which were all below 7 per cent.

Dependent children by Local Authority District and Council Area[3]

Maps 5.4, 5.5 and 5.6 show the geographical distribution of families with dependent children according to whether they belong to lone parent, married or cohabiting couple families. Generally, the majority of dependent children live in married couple families. As such, regions with a smaller proportion of married families with dependent children will generally have a larger proportion of lone parents or cohabiting couples with dependent children. It is important to bear in mind that the proportions are for all families with dependent children (not including other family types). As such, areas such as the South West, which has a large proportion of families with no children, may have smaller overall numbers of dependent children in any or all of the family types.

One method of investigating the prevalence of lone parent families is to calculate the proportion of all families they comprise. However, this is a generalised measure and it might be considered more appropriate to calculate the proportion of families with dependent children that are lone parent families. This is especially relevant since over 68 per cent of lone parent families in the UK have dependent children.[4]

Map 5.4 displays the proportions of lone parent families with dependent children of all families with dependent children for Local Authority Districts, District Council Areas, and Scottish Council Areas. For the sake of clarity, these three geographies will be referred to as areas.

Map **5.4**

Lone parent families with dependent children as a proportion of all families with dependent children, 2001

United Kingdom

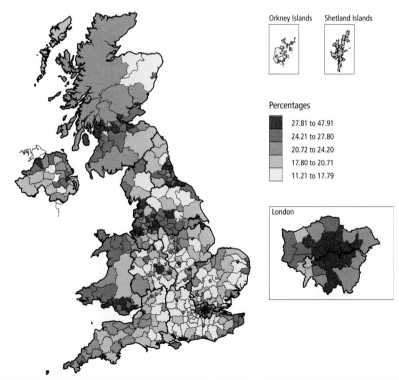

Orkney Islands   Shetland Islands

Percentages

- 27.81 to 47.91
- 24.21 to 27.80
- 20.72 to 24.20
- 17.80 to 20.71
- 11.21 to 17.79

London

Source: 2001 Census, Office for National Statistics; General Register Office for Scotland; Northern Ireland Statistics and Research Agency

Map **5.5**

Married couple families with dependent children as a proportion of all families with dependent children, 2001

United Kingdom

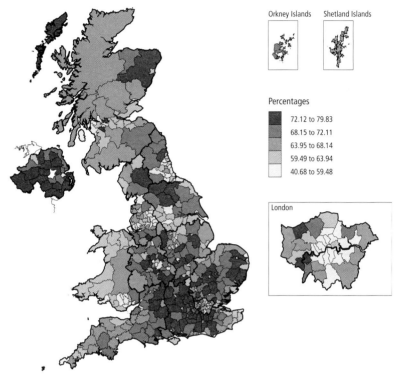

Map **5.6**

Cohabiting couple families with dependent children as a proportion of all families with dependent children, 2001

United Kingdom

Source: 2001 Census, Office for National Statistics; General Register Office for Scotland; Northern Ireland Statistics and Research Agency

It is possible to rank the areas to find the ten highest and ten lowest proportions. Lambeth has the highest proportion, 47.9 per cent, and is one of the six London districts in the highest ten. The remaining four areas are Manchester, Glasgow City, Liverpool and Belfast. The three areas with the lowest proportions are the Isles of Scilly, Wokingham and Chiltern.

Map 5.4 shows that lone parent families with dependent children are more likely to live in urban areas, or more specifically, the most populous urban areas in the UK.[5] The reasons for this may include a larger rate of partnership dissolution in urban areas.[6] Alternatively, it may be that lone parents are more likely to live in urban areas for economic reasons, which include housing and employment. Further research would be required to identify whether any of these explanations is correct.

As shown earlier (Map 5.2), the smallest proportion of lone parent families is in the East, South East and South West regions. To a certain extent, the lower prevalence of lone parent families in these regions is reflected in a lower likelihood of dependent children living in lone parent families.

Married couples with dependent children

The majority of dependent children in the UK, over 63 per cent, live in married couple families. However, as with other family types, there is a great deal of variation according to area. Map 5.5 shows that married couple families with dependent children are less likely to live in highly populated urban areas and is broadly the inverse of Map 5.4 (the same as Map 5.5, but for lone parent families). Having ranked the proportions of married couple families with dependent children (of all families with dependent children), eight of the lowest ten were also in the highest ten in Map 5.4. Of the highest ten in Map 5.5, five are in Northern Ireland. This is no doubt related to the overall high proportions of married families in Northern Ireland.

Cohabiting couples with dependent children

The proportions of cohabiting couples with dependent children as a proportion of all families with dependent children are illustrated in Map 5.6. The patterns shown are interesting because they do not conform to the general difference between urban and rural areas (as shown for lone parents and married couples). Families with dependent children are least likely to be cohabiting couple families in Northern Ireland. Again, this is probably owing to a greater prevalence of marriage, and a lower prevalence of cohabitation as a substitute.

It is more difficult to generalise about the location of areas with a high proportion of cohabiting couples with dependent children (of all families with dependent children). The ten areas with the highest proportion are (in order, highest first):

Norwich, Kingston upon Hull, Hyndburn, Great Yarmouth, Penwith, Bolsover, Swale, Rossendale, Brighton and Hove, and Easington. While there are no strong patterns to which these areas belong, there are pockets of high proportions clustered at a more generalised level. Locations where the proportions of dependent children families are more likely to be cohabiting couple families are: South West England, Mid and North Wales, Kent, Norfolk, Lincolnshire, Yorkshire, Lancashire, Durham, Tyne and Wear, and Moray.

It is interesting to note the relatively low proportions in London. Although London has a high incidence of cohabitation (Map 5.2), this is not associated with a high incidence of cohabiting families with dependent children. Cohabiting families in London are more likely to be without dependent children.

Families without dependent children

There are two main types of family with no dependent children: families with no (resident) children and families with non-dependent children only. In 2001, 41.1 per cent of families in the UK had no children and 15.3 per cent had non-dependent children only. The combination of these two family types represents over nine million families.

Generally, families with no children will be one of three types of married or cohabiting couple – younger couples who will have children in the future, couples who will never have children and couples whose children have left home. As such, families with no children may be at different stages in the life-course of a family.

Families with non-dependent children (only) are more likely to be at a specific stage in the life-course of a family. This is the stage before adult children move away from home or start their own family. However, there will be some exceptions to this. For example, an older childless adult (not in a couple) may continue or return to live with his or her parent(s) for care reasons. Nevertheless, a large number of the 2.5 million UK families with non-dependent children (only) contain children who will leave home or start their own families at some point in the future.

Lone parent families with non-dependent children only

Map 5.7 shows the distribution of lone parent families with non-dependent children only as a proportion of all families with non-dependent children only. Clearly there is a strong relationship between this proportion and geography: all of the ten areas with the highest proportion are in London. Looking at the map, most of the other areas with the highest proportions are found in the following generalised locations: Northern Ireland, London, West Scotland, Tyne and Wear,

Map **5.7**

Lone parent families with non-dependent children only as a proportion of all families with non-dependent children only, 2001

United Kingdom

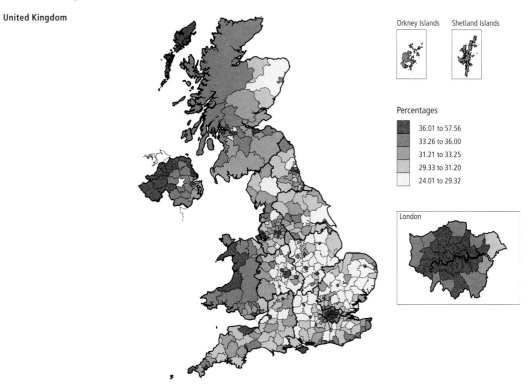

Map **5.8**

Cohabiting couple families with non-dependent children only as a proportion of all families with non-dependent children only, 2001

United Kingdom

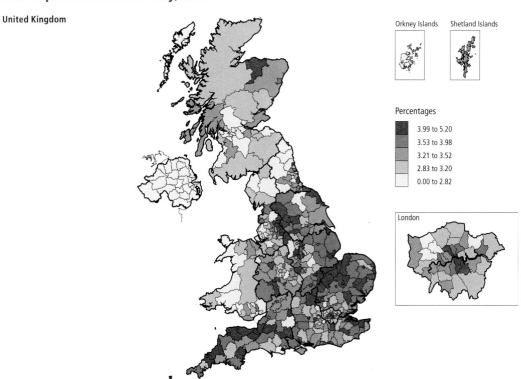

Source: 2001 Census, Office for National Statistics; General Register Office for Scotland; Northern Ireland Statistics and Research Agency

Greater Manchester, Merseyside, West Midlands, West Wales and the South East coast of England.

The areas with the lowest proportions are generally in the middle of England, particularly the East and the East and West Midlands. This is similar to the results shown in Map 5.4 for lone parents with dependent children. Both maps also show a general propensity for lone parent families to live in or around large urban centres, for example London, Glasgow, Belfast and Cardiff. However, the results for lone parents with non-dependent children only also show a variation between England, with low proportions outside urban centres, and the other three countries of the United Kingdom, with high proportions in non-urban areas.

Cohabiting couples with non-dependent children only

Compared with lone parents, there is a different overall pattern to the distribution of cohabiting couple families with non-dependent children only (as a proportion of all families with non-dependent children only – Map 5.8). Generally, in areas where there is a low proportion of lone parents with non-dependent children, there is a high proportion of equivalent cohabiting families. When considering Map 5.7 and Map 5.8 together, it should be remembered that the remaining proportion of families with non-dependent children only will relate to married couple families.

The highest proportions in Map 5.8 are in England, but not in the most populous urban areas. Norwich has the highest proportion, with 5.2 per cent and also has the highest proportion of cohabiting couples with dependent children (Map 5.6). The other areas with proportions over five per cent are Hyndburn, Milton Keynes, West Somerset, Pendle and Burnley.

Apart from the Isles of Scilly, all of the ten lowest proportions are in Northern Ireland. Previously, Map 5.2 showed the larger proportion of cohabiting couple families in England, which suggests that the lower proportions in Scotland, Wales and Northern Ireland are to be expected. Map 5.2 also showed high proportions of cohabiting families in London, but this is not shown in Map 5.8 (non-dependent children only) or Map 5.6 (dependent children). This is because cohabiting families in London are more likely to have no children.

Families with three or more dependent children

Map 5.9 shows the proportion of families with dependent children who have three or more children. Clearly, the majority of areas with the highest proportions are in Northern Ireland. The exception is Tower Hamlets, which has the highest proportion overall, 34.5 per cent. There are also a number of areas in London with high proportions, although the City of London has the lowest, 10.5 per cent.

Apart from Northern Ireland and London, areas with high proportions are in Wales, the Midlands, South East, South West and around Greater Manchester. The two main locations with the lowest proportions are South Scotland and North England. The three areas with the lowest proportions in Scotland are Falkirk, Renfrewshire and Aberdeen City. In England the three lowest are City of London, Chester-le-Street and Durham.

There will be many reasons for the variations in the proportion of large families (those with three or more dependent children). Variations in total fertility rates may explain why Northern Ireland has a larger proportion of large families.[7] However, it may be that particular areas are more affected by variations in age structure and associated age specific fertility rates.[8] Finally, it is known that fertility rates vary according to the mother's country of birth.[9] As such, areas with larger proportions of people from countries with high fertility might be expected to have a larger proportion of large families. Nevertheless, without further study the reasons for variations between areas are speculative.

Stepfamilies

The 2001 Census was the first census from which it is possible to calculate the number of stepfamilies and their type. In terms of family type there are two sorts of stepfamily: married and cohabiting. While it is possible for lone parent families to contain stepchildren, this is not included in the definition of a stepfamily in the 2001 Census.

Table 5.1 at the beginning of this chapter gives the figures for married and cohabiting stepfamilies. As with other family types, it is also possible to further split stepfamilies according to the presence or otherwise of dependent children. Nevertheless, the composition of stepfamilies, as distinct from non-stepfamilies, is of potentially greater interest. In other words, are there any children from the step-parent relationship (some children of both partners together)?

In 2001, there were over 876,000 stepfamilies in the UK, more than 5 per cent of all families. Table 5.10 shows that almost half of these had children from the female partner only, contrasting with only 8.2 per cent from the male partner only. This indicates a tendency for children to remain with their mother, rather than their father, when entering into stepfamily relationships (children of the male partner may live with their mother).

Northern Ireland shows the largest difference from the UK average. It has both a smaller proportion of stepfamilies where children are from the female partner only, 39.5 per cent, and a larger proportion of stepfamilies where children are from the male partner only, 9.5 per cent. London varies in the same direction with equivalent figures of 42.1 per cent and 10.7 per cent.

Map **5.9**

Families with three or more dependent children as a proportion of all families with dependent children, 2001

United Kingdom

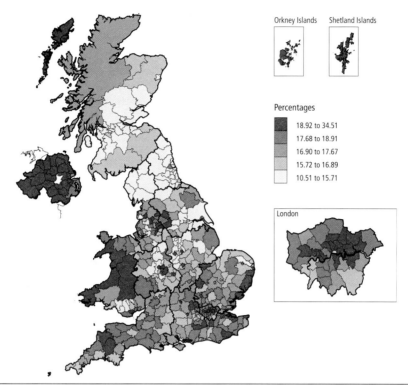

Source: 2001 Census, Office for National Statistics; General Register Office for Scotland; Northern Ireland Statistics and Research Agency

Table **5.10**

Proportion of stepfamilies according to stepchild status by Government Office Region and country, 2001

United Kingdom   Percentages

	Children of both partners, none together	Children of female partner only	Children of male partner only	Some children of both partners together
UK	3.2	49.6	8.2	39.0
North East	2.9	51.5	7.1	38.5
North West	3.2	49.2	7.6	40.0
Yorkshire and The Humber	3.2	50.9	7.5	38.5
East Midlands	3.7	51.0	8.2	37.1
West Midlands	3.3	48.1	8.3	40.3
East	3.3	51.5	7.9	37.2
London	3.0	42.1	10.7	44.1
South East	3.4	51.3	8.3	37.0
South West	3.5	51.8	7.5	37.2
Wales/Cymru	3.0	47.8	7.8	41.3
Scotland	2.8	51.7	8.2	37.3
Northern Ireland	2.4	39.5	9.5	48.6

Note: Percentages may not add up because of rounding.

Source: 2001 Census, Office for National Statistics; General Register Office for Scotland; Northern Ireland Statistics and Research Agency

In the UK, 39.0 per cent of stepfamilies had children from the new relationship but the majority of regions had a lower proportion than this. The exceptions were the North West, West Midlands, London, Wales and Northern Ireland, where 48.6 per cent of stepfamilies had children from the new relationship.

Stepfamilies with dependent children

Map 5.11 shows the proportion of all families with dependent children that are stepfamilies. The most striking feature of this map is the low proportions for Northern Ireland and the areas in and around London. The ten lowest proportions are all in Northern Ireland. The three lowest are, Dungannon, Cookstown and Magherafelt.

Hyndburn is the area with the highest proportion of families with dependent children that are stepfamilies, 14.9 per cent. Generally, it seems that areas with higher proportions are located next to the coast, in particular the east coast of England and the South West region.

When considering these results, it is important to consider the definition of a stepfamily with dependent children. A stepfamily is a couple family that contains at least one child who is not the child of both partners together. A dependent child stepfamily

must contain at least one child under 16 years old (or under 19 and in full-time education). The implication of these definitions is that there is likely to be a large variation in stepfamilies relating to the family history of their members. Step families may contain only one dependent child of one partner. On the other hand, they may contain children of a similar age from both partners (some together and/or some not) and older stepchildren who are non-dependent. It is therefore more difficult to generalise about stepfamilies than non-stepfamilies given the larger variety of inter-family relationships.

Married stepfamilies with dependent children

Map 5.12 shows the proportion of stepfamilies with dependent children that are married couple stepfamilies. A stepfamily is either headed by a married couple or a cohabiting couple. As such, the proportions of stepfamilies with dependent children that are cohabiting couple stepfamilies are opposite to those displayed in Map 5.12.

All of the ten areas with the highest proportions of married stepfamilies with dependent children (of all stepfamilies with dependent children) are in Northern Ireland. The area with the highest proportion is Armagh, with 75.0 per cent. Apart from

Map **5.11**

Stepfamilies with dependent children as a proportion of all families with dependent children[1], 2001

United Kingdom

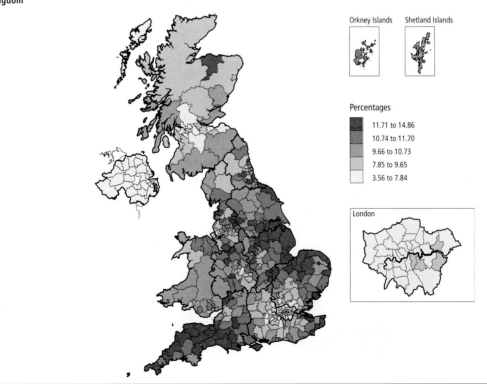

1 Figures for Westminster and City of London have been combined and are displayed under the boundary for Westminster.
  Figures for Penwith and the Isles of Scilly have been combined and are displayed under the boundary for Penwith.

Source: 2001 Census, Office for National Statistics; General Register Office for Scotland; Northern Ireland Statistics and Research Agency

Northern Ireland, the area with the highest proportion is Forest Heath (66.0 per cent). Other locations with high proportions include London (north and west), Richmondshire, Hart, Woking, Rutland and most of the areas in Wiltshire and West Sussex. In Wales, high proportions are in Bridgend, 60.9 per cent, and Pembrokeshire, 60.3 per cent. The area with the highest proportion in Scotland is Eilean Siar, also with 60.3 per cent.

Seven of the ten areas with the lowest proportions are in Scotland, which has low proportions in most areas. The area with the lowest proportion is East Ayrshire (44.0 per cent). Outside Scotland, the lowest proportions are in Tandridge (44.4 per cent), Hyndburn (45.7 per cent), Newcastle upon Tyne (47.0 per cent), West Somerset (47.8 per cent) and Nottingham (48.2 per cent). Other areas with low proportions are Kent, Cambridgeshire, and East Lancashire. Again, it should be noted that, by definition, these areas with a low proportion of married stepfamilies with dependent children have a high proportion of cohabiting stepfamilies with dependent children (of all stepfamilies with dependent children). The high and low proportions therefore represent one type of geographical variation in the patterns of marriage and cohabitation – that relating to stepfamilies.

It is interesting to note the differences between Map 5.12 and Map 5.5, which is the same as Map 5.12, but for all families rather than stepfamilies. Whereas Map 5.5 shows that in highly populated urban areas married couple families with dependent children are less prevalent (compared with other areas), Map 5.12 does not show the same for stepfamilies.

Stepfamilies with some children of both partners

Map 5.13 shows the proportion of stepfamilies with children of both partners together. The majority of the areas with the highest proportions are in Northern Ireland or London. The three areas with the highest proportions are Newry and Mourne (60.3 per cent), Strabane (57.7 per cent) and Derry (56.6 per cent). In London, the highest proportions are Tower Hamlets (55.8 per cent), Hackney (53.1 per cent) and Newham (52.9 per cent). Compared with the UK average, Wales also has high proportions with the three highest being Blaenau Gwent (45.3 per cent), Gwynedd (43.9 per cent) and Pembrokeshire (43.4 per cent).

The areas with low proportions are generally more rural areas. The five areas with the lowest proportions are Wychavon

Map **5.12**

Married stepfamilies with dependent children as a proportion of all stepfamilies with dependent children[1], 2001

United Kingdom

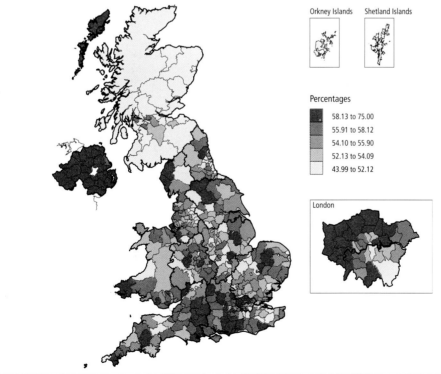

1 Figures for Westminster and City of London have been combined and are displayed under the boundary for Westminster.
  Figures for Penwith and the Isles of Scilly have been combined and are displayed under the boundary for Penwith.

Source: 2001 Census, Office for National Statistics; General Register Office for Scotland; Northern Ireland Statistics and Research Agency

Map **5.13**

Stepfamilies with some children of both partners together as a proportion of all stepfamilies[1], 2001

United Kingdom

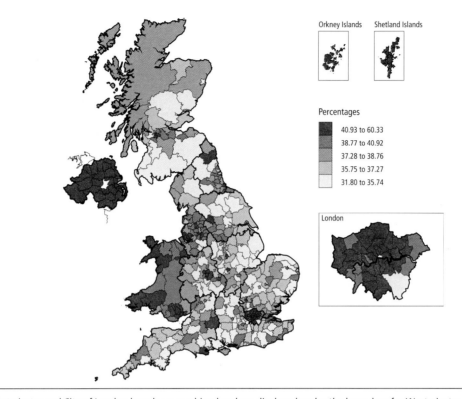

Orkney Islands   Shetland Islands

Percentages

- 40.93 to 60.33
- 38.77 to 40.92
- 37.28 to 38.76
- 35.75 to 37.27
- 31.80 to 35.74

London

1 Figures for Westminster and City of London have been combined and are displayed under the boundary for Westminster.
   Figures for Penwith and the Isles of Scilly have been combined and are displayed under the boundary for Penwith.

Source: 2001 Census, Office for National Statistics; General Register Office for Scotland; Northern Ireland Statistics and Research Agency

(31.8 per cent), Teesdale (32.1 per cent), Broadland (32.2 per cent), Hinckley and Bosworth (32.6 per cent) and Malvern Hills (32.7 per cent). Some areas in Scotland have low proportions, in particular Aberdeen City and Dumfries and Galloway (both 32.8 per cent). Also, despite the generally high proportions in London, only 34.5 per cent of stepfamilies in Bromley have children of both parents together.

Interpreting these geographical variations depends upon the differences between stepfamilies with or without children of both partners together. In the former, the couple will have some children together and some not, while in the latter, there will only be one or more children from previous relationships. Stepfamilies without children together might have formed more recently and not yet reached the decision to have a child together. However, this may not be the case and they may involve long-standing relationships. It is difficult to generalise about the history and composition of stepfamilies, but Map 5.13 does suggest geographical differences between the fertility behaviour of stepfamilies (with some children of both partners together). Areas with high proportions may simply reflect areas where families are more likely to have children. However, this conclusion cannot be confirmed without looking at completed family sizes and the fertility history of men and women in stepfamilies.

Multiple family households

While the majority of households in the 2001 Census contained only one family, a number of households contained more than one. These are referred to as multiple family households, and in the UK in 2001 there were 370,900. The detailed family type of each of these families is shown in the Appendix and more than half were married couple non-stepfamilies.

London has the largest number of families in multiple family households, almost 69,500. The smallest number is in Northern Ireland (11,450), closely followed by the North East (12,140). Broadly speaking, the proportions by family type for each country or GOR are fairly similar. Northern Ireland, Scotland, the North West and North East have a larger proportion of female lone parent families in multiple family households (all over 31 per cent). The East, South East and South West have a larger proportion of cohabiting non-stepfamilies (all over 16 per cent), whereas Northern Ireland has a very small proportion (5.2 per cent).

When considering the numbers of families in multiple family households for a particular geography, it is important to consider the total number of families. This is shown in Map 5.14, which provides an indication of the incidence of multiple family households.

London has the largest proportion of families in multiple family households (of all families). Six of the ten areas with the highest proportions are in London, the highest being Tower Hamlets and Brent (both with 7.8 per cent). Outside London, the other four are Slough (6.5 per cent), Leicester (5.6 per cent), Bradford and Birmingham (both 5.2 per cent). Of the next twenty areas with the highest proportions, thirteen are in London.

Of the areas with the lowest proportions, the majority are in the East and East Midlands regions, in the north of England and in Scotland. The three areas with the lowest proportions are Berwick-upon-Tweed (0.9 per cent), Scottish Borders and Angus (both with 1.0 per cent).

It may be considered that the proportion of families in multiple family households is a measure of housing need or possible overcrowding. To a certain extent this is reasonable, but the statistics do not show the reasons why families live in multiple family households. While it is true that the proportion of families in multiple family households may reflect the price and availability of housing, it may also reflect the disposition of the families in question. It is known that family size and the prevalence of multiple generation households varies according to ethnicity and religion.[10] Multiple family households may also exist in order that families can share resources or the responsibilities of caring for dependents.

Lone parent families in multiple family households

As suggested above (and shown in the Appendix), the proportion of lone parent families in multiple family households varies by country and GOR. Map 5.15 shows how the proportion of lone parent families varies by area, but the proportion is the number in multiple family households as a proportion of all lone parent families. In other words, Map 5.15 shows the proportion of all lone parent families that are families in multiple family households.

Seven of the ten highest proportions are in Northern Ireland, including Limavady (9.7 per cent), Derry, Magherafelt and Carrickfergus (all three with 7.5 per cent). The three outside Northern Ireland are Tower Hamlets (9.3 per cent), Slough (7.5 per cent) and Bradford (7.2 per cent).

Areas with low proportions are found throughout the UK (apart from Northern Ireland). Norwich has the lowest (2.2 per

Map **5.14**

Families in multiple family households as a proportion of all families[1], 2001

United Kingdom

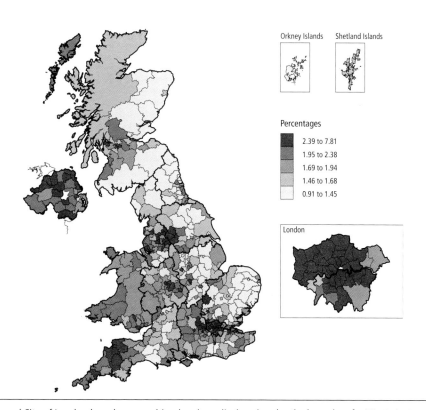

Percentages

■	2.39 to 7.81
▨	1.95 to 2.38
▨	1.69 to 1.94
▨	1.46 to 1.68
□	0.91 to 1.45

1 Figures for Westminster and City of London have been combined and are displayed under the boundary for Westminster.
  Figures for Penwith and the Isles of Scilly have been combined and are displayed under the boundary for Penwith.

Source: 2001 Census, Office for National Statistics; General Register Office for Scotland; Northern Ireland Statistics and Research Agency

Map **5.15**

Lone parent families in multiple family households as a proportion of all lone parent families[1], 2001

United Kingdom

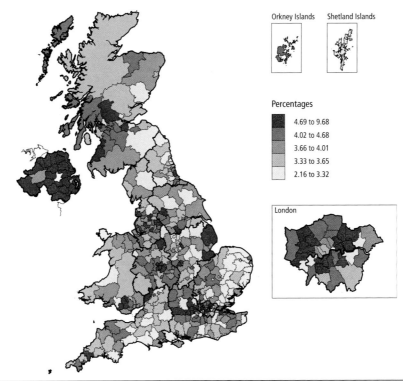

Orkney Islands Shetland Islands

Percentages

- 4.69 to 9.68
- 4.02 to 4.68
- 3.66 to 4.01
- 3.33 to 3.65
- 2.16 to 3.32

London

1 Figures for Westminster and City of London have been combined and are displayed under the boundary for Westminster.
Figures for Penwith and the Isles of Scilly have been combined and are displayed under the boundary for Penwith.

Source: 2001 Census, Office for National Statistics; General Register Office for Scotland; Northern Ireland Statistics and Research Agency

cent), followed by Cambridge, Barking and Dagenham, Braintree, Eastbourne and Harlow (all 2.4 per cent).

Apart from Northern Ireland's high proportions, Map 5.15 does not have a very distinct geographical pattern. Of the previous maps, it is most similar to Map 5.14. This implies that the variation in the distribution of multiple family households is the main driver of the geographical variations in lone parents in multiple family households (Map 5.15).

Notes and References

1 See Population Estimates for UK, England and Wales, Scotland and Northern Ireland, available at:
www.statistics.gov.uk/statbase/Product.asp?vlnk=601&More=N

2 Quantiles are less susceptile to long tailed distributions and outliers, (values that are isolated from the bulk of the responses).

3 Local Authority District for England and Wales, District Council Areas for Northern Ireland and Council Areas for Scotland.

4 See Chapter 1, Table 1.3.

5 See Map 3.2 in Office for National Statistics (2005) *Focus on People and Migration*, Palgrave Macmillan: Basingstoke, available at:
www.statistics.gov.uk/statbase/Product.asp?vlnk=12899

6 Boyle PJ, Kulu H, Cooke T, Gayle V and Mulder CH (2006) *The effect of moving on union dissolution*, Max Planck Institute for Demographic Research, MPIDR Working Paper: Rostock

7 NISRA (2005) Registrar General Annual Report, Births Comparison with other Countries of the United Kingdom 1981–2005, available at:
www.nisra.gov.uk/archive/demography/publications/annual_reports/2005/Table1.10c_2005.xls

8 Office for National Statistics (2005) *Focus on people and migration*, Palgrave Macmillan: Basingstoke, Figure 5.6, available at:
www.statistics.gov.uk/statbase/Product.asp?vlnk=12899

9 Office for National Statistics (2005) *Focus on people and migration*, Palgrave Macmillan: Basingstoke, Figure 5.13, available at:
www.statistics.gov.uk/statbase/Product.asp?vlnk=12899

10 See Office for National Statistics (2006) *Focus on Ethnicity and Religion*, Palgrave Macmillan: Basingstoke, in particular Chapter 4: 'Households and Families', pp 83–110.

Appendix

Chapter 2: Unpaid care and the family

The 2001 Census

The 2001 Census question on unpaid care asks:

> Do you look after, or give any help or support to family members, friends, neighbours, or others because of:
>
> • Long-term physical or mental ill-health or disability, or
>
> • problems relating to old age?
>
> *Do not count anything you do as part of your paid employment*
>
> *Time spent in a typical week*
>
> • No
>
> • Yes, 1 – 19 hours a week
>
> • Yes, 20 – 49 hours a week
>
> • Yes, 50+ hours a week

This question records whether a person gives any help or support to family members, friends, neighbours or others because of long-term physical or mental ill-health or disability, or problems related to old age. Note that there is no specific reference to whether this care is provided within the household or outside the household. Therefore, no explicit link can be created to infer that the individual providing care is providing it to a person within the same household.

Information derived from answers to the 2001 Census question on unpaid care is analysed in this chapter using two different types of source. First, where possible, the data uses information derived from tables specially commissioned by the author from the Office for National Statistics. These tables provide aggregated, anonymised data on provision of unpaid care for the total enumerated population and cover topics including provision of care by marital status, partnership status, ethnic group and economic activity. The analyses using the commissioned tables, reported here, relate to the population in Great Britain, with the exception of the tables showing ethnic group which relate to the population in England and Wales.

Second, the chapter uses the Licensed 3% Individual Sample of Anonymised Records (SAR) from the 2001 Census. The Licensed Individual SAR contains 1.8 million records, representing 3% of the enumerated population of England, Wales, Scotland and Northern Ireland. Key variables used in this chapter to analyse provision of care, which derive from the Individual SAR include: family type, ethnic group and health.

Data on provision of informal care in the 2000/01 General Household Survey (GHS)

The 2001 Census data are illuminated in the chapter on unpaid care and the family by reference to secondary analyses of the 2000/01 General Household Survey (GHS) data on provision of informal care. The GHS is a multipurpose continuous survey based on a large sample of the general population resident in private (non-institutional) households in Great Britain. Questions on the provision of informal care were included in 1985, 1990, 1995 and 2000. The analysis reported here uses data from the 2000 GHS.

In the 2000 GHS approximately 14,000 people aged 16 and over throughout the country responded to the questions on informal care. Respondents in the 2000 GHS were asked the questions on informal care shown in the box below. They were also asked for information on the number of hours per week for which care was provided and other information on care provision, including the locus of care and the relationship of the care-recipient to the care-provider.

The 2000/01 GHS question on unpaid care asks:

> I'd like to talk now about caring informally for others.
>
> Some people have extra responsibilities because they look after someone who has long term physical or mental ill health or disability, or problems related to old age.
>
> .... May I check, is there anyone living with you who is sick, disabled or elderly whom you look after or give special help to, other than in a professional capacity (for example, a sick or disabled (or elderly) relative/husband/wife/child/friend/ parent etc)?
>
> ... Is there anyone (either living with you or not living with you) who is sick, disabled or elderly whom you look after or give special help to, other than in a professional capacity (for example, a sick or disabled (or elderly) relative/husband/ wife/child/ friend/parent etc)?

For more information on informal care and the GHS see:

Office for National Statistics (2002) *Carers 2000*, TSO: London, available at: www.statistics.gov.uk/downloads/theme_health/ carers2000.pdf

Comparison of the 2001 Census and 2000/01 GHS data on unpaid/informal care

The 2001 Census and the 2000/01 GHS both collect information on provision of unpaid or informal care. The numbers and proportions of people providing unpaid care, however, are lower in the Census than in the GHS (Table A1). One reason for this is

Table **A1**

Provision of unpaid care by the adult[1] population in households, 2001 Census and 2000/01 GHS

Great Britain

(numbers in thousands and percentages)

	2001 Census	GHS (weighted numbers)
People providing unpaid care[2]	5,478	6,584
Total population[3]	42,637	40,657
Proportion providing unpaid care	13%	16%

1 People aged 19 and over.
2 Provision of care in the 2001 Census is defined as one or more hour(s) a week; provision of care in the GHS includes people providing care for less than an hour a week.
3 Total population in private households. Total numbers are lower in the 2000/01 GHS weighted base than in the 2001 Census population partly because the GHS carers data exclude missing answers from the weighted base.

Source: 2001 Census, Office for National Statistics; 2000/01 GHS (weighted sample)

that the GHS asks about all informal care whereas the Census asks about care provided for one hour or more.

Comparison of care for 20 hours a week in the 20001 Census and 2000/01 GHS

The proportion of the population providing care for 20 hours a week or more is similar in both the 2001 Census and the 2000/01 GHS. Both show that around 4 per cent of the population aged 19 and over provide unpaid or informal care for 20 hours a week or more (Figure A2). There are, however, differences in the proportion of the adult population providing care between

the 2001 Census and the 2000/01 GHS using other indicators of intensity (hours of care). The proportion providing care for 20 to 49 hours a week is lower in the Census than the GHS, while the proportion providing care for 50 hours a week or more is higher in the Census than in the GHS.

The more detailed table (Table A3) below shows the lower and upper confidence intervals for the proportion of the adult population providing care for 20 hours a week or more derived from the GHS sample. The table shows that the proportion of the population providing care for 20 hours a week or more, derived from the 2001 Census, lies between the lower and upper confidence intervals for the proportion of the population providing care for 20 hours a week or more, derived from the 2000/01 GHS.

Table **A3**

Proportion of the adult population providing care for long hours, 2001 Census and 2000/01 GHS

Great Britain

Percentage

	Census	GHS	GHS lower confidence interval[1]	GHS upper confidence interval[1]
20–49	1.44	2.65	2.39	2.94
50+	2.78	1.82	1.61	2.1
20+	4.22	4.32	4.13	4.83

1 These are 95 per cent confidence intervals.

Source: 2001 Census, Office for National Statistics; 2000/01 GHS (unweighted sample = 13,540)

Figure **A2**

Proportion of the adult population providing care for long hours, 2001 Census and 2000/01 GHS

Great Britain

Percentages

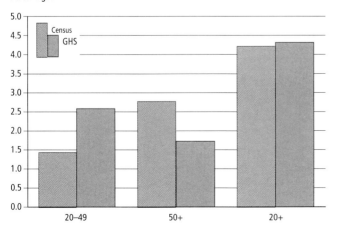

Source: 2001 Census, Office for National Statistics; 2000/01 GHS (weighted base (000's) = 40,657, unweighted sample = 13,540)

Relationship of care-recipient to care-giver

Secondary analyses of the 2000/01 GHS, prepared for the chapter on unpaid care, focus in particular on who care is provided for, since it seems important to identify care provided for different family members. People providing care in the GHS may care for up to six care-recipients. The description of the relationship of care-recipients to care-givers, used here, employs a derived variable, made available as part of the GHS dataset, which combines relationships, so that each carer is allocated to one combination only. Combinations for spouses, for example, include 'spouse only and 'spouse and others'. These combinations have been further combined here to yield a four-fold classification of relationship of care-recipient to care-giver: spouse/partner, parent-in-law, child and other. The category, care for a spouse, for example, includes both care for a spouse and care for a spouse and others.

Chapter 3: Family structure and family formation – education as outcome and explanation

Additional information for Table 3.3b

Table A4 below is a repeat of Table 3.3b, but includes the base numbers.

Table **A4**

Single individuals who are not lone parents, are aged 17, and are living within families by family type and sex: percentages in full-time education, 2001

Great Britain   Percentages

	Male			Female	
	Percentage	Base		Percentage	Base
Married couple non-stepfamily	68.9	204,078		77.9	188,648
Married couple stepfamily	53.5	25,196		65.8	22,991
Cohabiting couple non-stepfamily	50.6	5,316		63.7	4,632
Cohabiting couple stepfamily	49.5	14,522		63.4	13,069
Lone parent family (male)	53.2	14,288		64.9	10,432
Lone parent family (female)	58.5	63,141		69.3	61,655

Source: 2001 Census, Office for National Statistics, General Register Office for Scotland

Chapter 4: Family living arrangements and health

Additional factors for Table 4.6

In Chapter 4, Table 4.6 shows on average the increased chance of being in a higher risk (poorer health) category after controlling for age, compared with individuals who are married. Table A5 below shows data for five further health indicators.

Table A5

Relative risk of health problem by marital status (married = 1), by age and sex, 2001

England

	Age group 20–64		Age group 65 and over	
	Men	Women	Men	Women
Perceived lack of social support				
Single	1.33*	1.27*	1.40*	1.57*
Separated	1.56*	1.29*	1.13	1.03
Divorced	1.42*	1.39*	1.51*	0.85
Widowed	1.22	1.11	0.90	0.94
Cohabiting	1.02	1.01	0.98	1.56*
Hypertensive				
Single	1.21*	1.29*	1.35*	0.93
Separated	0.98	0.91	1.39*	0.90
Divorced	0.92	0.94	1.12	0.96
Widowed	1.12	1.07	1.11*	0.98
Cohabiting	0.98	0.97	0.75	1.04
Acute illness in last 2 weeks				
Single	1.02	1.15	1.04	0.87
Separated	1.39	1.13	1.68	1.43
Divorced	1.52*	1.48*	1.57*	1.36
Widowed	1.58*	1.19	0.93	1.31*
Cohabiting	1.14	1.07	NA	0.51
General health				
Single	1.46*	1.46*	1.14	0.78
Separated	1.45*	1.56*	1.41	0.81
Divorced	1.47*	1.66*	1.41*	1.29*
Widowed	1.24	1.56*	1.08	1.03
Cohabiting	1.10	1.12	0.77	0.88
Alcohol consumption				
Single	1.40*	1.61*	0.77	0.27*
Separated	1.57*	1.23	1.03	0.79
Divorced	1.35*	1.12	1.14	0.60
Widowed	1.15	0.80	1.37*	0.77
Cohabiting	1.31*	1.48*	1.09	2.76*

Notes: * statistically significantly different from 1.0 at 95% level.
Models control for age by including linear and quadratic age terms (not shown).

Source: 2001 HSE

Additional factors for Table 4.8

In Chapter 4, Table 4.8 shows on average the increased chance of being in a higher risk (poorer health) category after controlling for age, compared with individuals who are with a partner and have no child(ren). Table A6 below shows data for five further health indicators.

Table A6

Relative risk of health problem by family type (with partner and no child(ren) = 1), by age and sex, 2001

England

	Age group 20–64		Age group 65 and over	
	Men	Women	Men	Women
Perceived lack of social support				
No partner, no child	1.42*	1.23*	1.13	0.99
No partner, child	1.30*	1.73*	0.71	0.98
Partner and child	1.07	1.23*	1.07	1.24
Hypertensive				
No partner, no child	1.07	1.11	1.16*	0.96
No partner, child	0.95	0.86	1.26*	1.05
Partner and child	0.92	0.96	1.05	1.01
Acute illness in last 2 weeks				
No partner, no child	0.99	1.28*	1.08	1.29*
No partner, child	1.40	1.10	1.15	1.28
Partner and child	0.78*	0.94	0.53	1.00
General health				
No partner, no child	1.42*	1.48*	1.17*	1.02
No partner, child	1.31	1.57*	1.42*	1.30*
Partner and child	0.98	0.98	1.16	1.23
Alcohol consumption				
No partner, no child	1.15*	1.15*	1.20	0.65*
No partner, child	1.32*	0.64*	0.48	0.42*
Partner and child	0.81*	0.60*	0.70	0.13*

Notes: * statistically significantly different from 1.0 at 95% level.
Models control for age by including linear and quadratic age terms (not shown).

Source: 2001 HSE

Chapter 5: Family Geography

The following tables show complete results for GOR and
country as referred to in Chapter five.

Table A7

Families by child status, 2001

United Kingdom   Percentages

	One dependent child	Two dependent children	Three or more dependent children	No children	Non-dependent children only
UK	18.7	17.3	7.7	41.1	15.3
North East	20.4	17.0	6.6	39.4	16.7
North West	19.8	17.3	7.9	38.6	16.4
Yorkshire and The Humber	18.7	17.2	7.5	42.0	14.5
East Midlands	17.9	17.2	7.1	43.7	14.1
West Midlands	18.9	17.0	8.1	40.2	15.9
East	16.8	17.4	7.5	44.2	14.1
London	21.0	17.6	9.3	35.9	16.2
South East	17.0	17.5	7.5	44.2	13.8
South West	16.4	16.6	6.9	46.9	13.2
Wales/Cymru	19.1	17.0	7.5	40.4	16.0
Scotland	20.0	17.0	6.4	39.6	17.1
Northern Ireland	20.3	18.6	12.8	28.7	19.6

Note: Percentages may not add up because of rounding.

Source: 2001 Census, Office for National Statistics; General Register Office for Scotland; Northern Ireland Statistics and Research Agency

Table A8

Number of families in multiple family households by type of family, 2001

United Kingdom   Percentages

	Lone parent family (male)	Lone parent family (female)	Married couple non-stepfamily	Married couple stepfamily	Cohabiting couple non-step family	Cohabiting couple step family
UK	4.6	24.7	53.9	2.7	12.9	1.1
North East	4.8	35.4	46.3	2.1	10.2	1.2
North West	4.6	31.5	50.0	2.5	10.3	1.1
Yorkshire and The Humber	5.0	25.1	54.9	3.2	10.6	1.3
East Midlands	4.6	23.2	56.7	2.5	11.9	1.1
West Midlands	4.6	23.3	58.9	3.2	9.0	1.0
East	4.4	22.6	53.2	2.6	16.2	1.2
London	4.9	22.7	55.3	2.9	13.2	1.0
South East	4.3	21.6	53.2	2.3	17.4	1.2
South West	4.3	22.1	53.1	2.3	16.9	1.4
Wales/Cymru	5.0	29.8	50.2	2.4	11.4	1.2
Scotland	5.1	36.4	45.9	1.9	9.8	0.9
Northern Ireland	5.0	43.2	44.2	1.7	5.2	0.8

Note: Percentages may not add up because of rounding.

Source: 2001 Census, Office for National Statistics; General Register Office for Scotland; Northern Ireland Statistics and Research Agency

Glossary

Administrative geographies

Administrative geographies are the hierarchy of areas relating to national and local government in the UK. For example: Government Office Regions and Unitary Authorities in England; Council Areas in Scotland and District Council Areas in Northern Ireland.

Adults

In the 2001 Census an adult is someone who is not classified as a dependent child (see: *Dependent child*). However, in Chapter Two: 'Unpaid care and the family', adults are defined as people aged 19 or over, unless otherwise stated.

Cohabiting

See: *Living arrangements*

Cohort

A group of people with a common experience, who are observed through time. For example the cohort of people born in 1970.

Commissioned Tables

Users can ask for particular tables to be run from the 2001 Census. These commissioned tables are available on request. See www.statistics.gov.uk/census2001/access_results.asp. Some of the analysis in this volume is based on commissioned tables.

Communal establishment

Defined in the 2001 Census as 'providing managed residential accommodation'. People were assumed to be 'resident' in a communal establishment if they had been living, or intended to live there, for six months or more. Communal establishments cover universities and colleges, hospitals, hostels and homes, some hotels and guest houses (with capacity for ten or more people), holiday complexes, defence establishments (but not married quarters) and prisons.

Council area

The 1994 Local Government (Scotland) Act led to the abolition of the existing structure of nine regions and 53 districts, although the three island councils remained. Since April 1996 Scotland has been divided into 32 council areas, whose councils are unitary administrations with responsibility for all areas of local government.

Dependent child

Defined in the Census, the Labour Force Survey and the General Household Survey, as a child living with their parent(s) aged under 16, or aged 16 to 18 in full-time education, excluding all children who have a spouse, partner or child living in the household.

District council areas

See: *Local government district*

Economic activity

In Chapter Two: 'Unpaid care and the family', a three-fold classification of economic activity is used: employed full-time, employed part-time and not in paid work (including unemployed and economically inactive).

Ethnic group

The information for the ethnic group of each respondent is based on the data and categorisation generated from the 2001 Census from the Office for National Statistics, the General Register Office for Scotland and the Northern Ireland Statistics and Research Agency.

In both 1991 and 2001 respondents were asked to which ethnic group they considered themselves to belong. The question in 2001 had more extensive categories than those of 1991 so people could tick 'Mixed' for the first time. This change in answer categories may account for a small part of the observed increase in the minority ethnic population over the period.

Different versions of the ethnic group question were asked in England and Wales, in Scotland and in Northern Ireland, to reflect local differences in the requirement for information. However, results are comparable across the UK as a whole.

Extended family household

See: *Household types*

Family

A married or cohabiting couple, with or without their never-married child or children (of any age), including couples with no children and lone parents with their never-married child or children. A family could also consist of a grandparent or grandparents with grandchild or grandchildren if the parents of the grandchild or grandchildren are not usually resident in the household. In the 2001 Census, less than one per cent of all families were a grandparent family. In the GHS and Census, cohabiting couple families include same-sex couples where the respondents choose to identify themselves.

Family Reference Person (FRP)

FRP is used to identify a family and its characteristics. In a lone-parent family the FRP is taken to be the lone parent. In the 2001 Census the FRP in a couple is based on economic activity, then age (oldest), then the first member of the couple on the Census form.

Full-time student

Defined in the 2001 Census as a person responding 'yes' to the question 'Are you a schoolchild or student in full-time education?'.

Further education

Full- or part-time education for people over compulsory school age. Further education is taught in a variety of settings including further education colleges, schools and work-based training.

General Household Survey (GHS)

The General Household Survey (GHS) is an inter-departmental multi-purpose continuous survey carried out by ONS that collects information on a range of topics from people living in private households in Great Britain. The survey has run continuously since 1971, except for breaks in 1997/8 (when the survey was reviewed) and 1999/2000 when the survey was re-developed.

Government Office Region (GOR)

Areas in England for which regional government offices are responsible. GORs were adopted in 1996 as the government's statistical regions.

Health Survey for England (HSE)

An annual survey of households in England commissioned by the Department of Health.

Household

A person living alone or a group of people who have the same address as their only or main residence and with common housekeeping. For example, the 2001 Census defined this as those who either share one meal a day or share the living accommodation. Although definitions differ slightly across surveys and the census, they are broadly similar. Households exclude people living in communal establishments.

Household Reference Person (HRP)

HRP is used to identify a household and its characteristics. In the 2001 Census, HRP replaces Head of Household, which was used in 1991. A person living alone is the HRP. If the household contains only one family (with or without ungrouped individuals) the HRP is the same as the Family Reference Person (FRP). If there is more than one family in the household, the HRP is chosen from among the FRPs using the same criteria as for choosing the FRP. If there is no family, the HRP is chosen from the individuals using the same criteria. In 1991, the Head of Household was taken as the first person on the form unless that person was aged under 16 or was not usually resident in the household.

Household types

Households with more than one person can include one family, ungrouped individuals who may or may not be related to each other, and/or any additional families in the household.

Extended family households are defined as a family plus other related individuals, or more than one family with or without other individuals (either the families or the individuals must be related to each other in some way). They can also consist of a group of related individuals who are not in a family, for instance a pair of adult siblings living in the same household.

Multi-family households are defined as households containing more than one family.

Multi-person households are defined as two or more people who are either not related or are related but do not form a family.

Multi-generational households are one type of extended family household that contain either: three or more generations if it includes a lone parent family or a couple with children, or two generations including a couple with no children or multiple family units that also include further generations.

Individual Sample of Anonymised Records (ISAR or SAR)

Abstract of individual census records, made available with strictly protected confidentiality. SARs are known more commonly in other countries as 'census microdata' or 'public use samples'.

Labour Force Survey (LFS)

A quarterly sample survey of households living at private addresses in Great Britain. Its purpose is to provide information on the UK labour market that can be used to develop, manage, evaluate and report on labour market policies. The survey seeks information on respondents' personal circumstances and their labour market status during a specific reference period, usually of one or four weeks (depending on the topic), immediately prior to the interview.

Limiting long-term illness

Limiting long-term illness covers any long-term illness, health problem or disability that limits daily activities or work a person can do.

Living arrangements

This is an ONS harmonised survey classification and applies to all people in households. In the 2001 Census, living arrangements are calculated by combining the responses to the question on legal marital status (see: *Marital status*) and the responses to the relationship question (see: *Relationship matrix*). In the GHS and LFS, living arrangements are asked directly in the questionnaires.

One of the main reasons for analysing living arrangements is so that cohabiting couples can be identified. It should be noted that cohabiting couples may be married or have any other marital status (see: *Marital status*).

Local authority district

The lower level of local government within the two-tier structure that has remained in parts of England since local government reorganisation.

Local government district

Replaced Northern Ireland's two tier administrative structure in October 1973. Outside Northern Ireland, the 26 local government districts are known as 'district council areas'. They are unitary administrations and are responsible for all areas of local government, but their remit is more limited than that of local authorities in the rest of the UK.

London boroughs

The local government areas of Greater London. The borough councils are unitary administrations with a status similar to metropolitan districts, except that they are affected by policies implemented by the Greater London Authority (GLA). There are 32 London boroughs, but the City of London (which has a different legal status) is often considered as a borough for statistical purposes. The London boroughs and the City of London together cover the whole Greater London area.

Lone parent family

Defined in the 2001 Census as a father or mother together with his or her child or children, providing that the children do not have a spouse, partner or child in the household. Also can encompass a grandparent with grandchild(ren) where there are no children in the intervening generation in the household.

The LFS definition is a lone parent, living with his or her never-married children, providing that these children have no children of their own living with them.

The GHS definition is one parent, irrespective of sex, living with his or her never-married dependent children, provided these children have no children of their own. Married or cohabiting women with dependent children, whose partners are not defined as resident in the household, are not classified as one-parent families because it is known that the majority

of them are only temporarily separated from their husbands for a reason that does not imply the breakdown of the marriage (for example, because the husband usually works away from home).

Longitudinal study

Although definitions can vary, a longitudinal study is generally a survey where the same respondents are measured repeatedly over time. For example, the same sample (or panel) of older people may be surveyed every year for a longitudinal study of aging. Longitudinal data are preferable to *pseudo cohort data* when analysing how individuals change over time.

Marital status

Usually refers to the legal marital status of an individual or couple (*de jure*). In the 2001 Census available responses were: single (never married), married (first marriage), remarried, separated (but still legally married), divorced, or widowed.

Since 1996 the GHS has asked separate questions at the beginning of the questionnaire to identify the legal marital status and living arrangements of respondents in the household. The latter includes a category for cohabiting. Before 1996, unrelated adults of the opposite sex were classified as cohabiting if they considered themselves to be living together as a couple. From 1996, they have been recorded as same sex couples.

More recently, the introduction of Civil Partnerships has expanded the possible responses to questions on legal marital status. The 2007 LFS available responses are: single (never married); married (living with husband/wife); married (separated from husband/wife); divorced; widowed; a civil partner in a legally-recognised Civil Partnership; in a legally-recognised Civil Partnership and separated from his/her civil partner; formerly a civil partner; the Civil Partnership now legally dissolved; or a surviving civil partner: his/her partner having since died.

For more information on cohabiting and actual (*de facto*) marital status, see: *Living arrangements*

Median age

The midpoint age that separates the younger half of a population from the older half.

Mixed ethnic group

Includes the 'White and Black Caribbean', 'White and Black African', 'White and Asian' and 'Other Mixed' ethnic groups.

Mortality

Refers to death and statistics for the number or rate of deaths, as opposed to *Morbidity.*

Mortality rates

Mortality rates are used to control for population size when studying deaths. A simple mortality rate would take the number of deaths and divide by the total population for which those deaths apply. For example, all deaths to women divided by the population of all women.

Morbidity

Refers to disease and statistics for the number or rate of diseases, as opposed to *Mortality*.

Multi-family households

See *Household types*

Multi-person household

See: *Household types*

Multi-generational household

See: *Household types*

National Statistics Socio-economic classification (NSSEC)

From April 2001 the National Statistics Socio-economic Classification (NSSEC) was introduced for all official statistics and surveys. It replaced Social Class based on occupation and Socio-economic Groups (SEG).

NSSEC categories are broadly defined as follows:

Classes 1 and 2: managerial and professional occupations

Classes 3, 4 and 5: intermediate occupations, small employers, own account workers, lower supervisory and technical occupations

Classes 6 and 7: semi-routine and routine occupations

Full details can be found in 'The National Statistics Socio-economic Classification User Manual 2002', ONS 2002.

Non-dependent children

Children aged 16 and over living with their parent(s) who have no spouse, partner or child living in the household. The definition excludes those aged 16 to 18 in full-time education (see: *Dependent children*).

Non-White

People from all ethnic groups other than the 'White British', 'White Scottish', 'White Irish', 'White Other British' and 'Other White' groups.

Pensioner/retirement age

Age 65 and older for men and age 60 and older for women.

Pseudo cohort analysis

Analysis that uses survey data for different years, where different individuals are surveyed each year. The results from different years are then combined to create a time series of data. From this, results can be obtained for particular cohorts (for example, those born in 1970). The results do not represent a true cohort because the individuals being surveyed are not the same for each year.

Qualifications

In the 2001 Census, the highest level of qualifications variable uses both the educational and vocational qualifications question and the professional qualifications question. This enables the following categories to be calculated:

No qualifications: no academic or professional qualifications.

Level 1: one or more 'O' levels/CSEs/GCSEs (any grade); NVQ level 1; Foundation GNVQ; or equivalents.

Level 2: five or more 'O' levels; 5+ CSEs (grade 1); five or more GCSEs (grade A – C); 1+ 'A' levels/'AS' levels; NVQ level 2; Intermediate GNVQ; or equivalents.

Level 3: two or more 'A' levels; four or more 'AS' levels; Higher School Certificate; NVQ level 3; Advanced GNVQ; or equivalents.

Level 4/5: First degree; Higher Degree; NVQ levels 4-5; HNC; HND; Qualified Teacher Status; Qualified Medical Doctor; Qualified Dentist; Qualified Nurse, Midwife, Health Visitor; or equivalents.

Other qualifications/level unknown: other qualifications (for example, City and Guilds); other professional qualification.

Quantiles

A general term for the method of dividing data into equal parts (see: *Quintiles*).

Quintiles

The quintiles of a distribution divide it into fifths. Thus the upper quintile (upper category) of a distribution of household income is the level of income that is expected by 20% of the households in the distribution. 20% of the households have an income less than the lower quintile so it follows that 60% of the households have an income between the upper and lower quintiles.

Relationship matrix/Relationship grid

A major change in the information collected about households and families was the introduction of the relationship matrix question in the GHS in 1993. The new question asked about

536934

the relationship of every household member to every other household member rather than just the head of household as was previously the case. The relationship matrix question is now used in the LFS and was used in the 2001 census. In addition to identifying nuclear family units, the matrix enables us to group individuals in different ways. For example, extended families and other relationships outside the nuclear family unit can be recognised.

Relative risk

This measures risk relative to a benchmark. For example, in Chapter Four: 'Family living arrangements and health', the relative risk of health problems is given. In Table 6 of this chapter, the benchmark is married individuals, who are given a value of 1.0 for all measures of health. All other values in the table are then compared with married individuals so that values greater than 1.0 have a greater risk and vice versa.

SAR

See: *Individual Sample of Anonymised Records*

Scottish council area

See: *Council area*

Stepfamilies

A stepfamily is one where there is at least one child who belongs to only one member of a married or cohabiting couple. A non-stepfamily is one where all children are children of both members of a married or cohabiting couple. Any parent living on their own with children is classified as a lone parent.

By definition a stepfamily must contain children. In some cases, although a stepfamily may be classified as a stepfamily with dependent children, the dependent children may not be stepchildren. In this example, there will be non-dependent stepchildren who cause the family to be classified as a stepfamily.

The family information section of the GHS is the main source that can identify stepfamilies and stepchildren. Analysis can be carried out for families headed by those aged 16 to 59. The 2001 Census was the first census that allowed the identification of stepfamilies (because of the relationship matrix) and is the only current source which can provide detailed information about stepfamilies and the children living in them.

Unitary authority

Area with a single tier of local government (as opposed to the two-tier county: district structure). In practice, the term is applied only to the 22 UAs established in Wales in 1996, and the 46 UAs established of England between 1995 and 1998. However, London boroughs and metropolitan districts in England, council

areas in Scotland and district council areas in Northern Ireland are all also served by single-tier (unitary) administrations.

Unpaid care

The term 'unpaid care' covers any unpaid help looking after, or supporting, family members, friends, neighbours or others because of their long-term physical or mental ill-health or disability or problems related to old age.

White

The term 'White' refers to individuals from the 'White British', 'White Scottish', 'White Irish', 'White Other British' and 'Other White' ethnic groups.

Working age

People aged between 16 and state pension age (currently age 65 and over for men and age 60 and over for women).

Young adults

People aged 16 to 24.